FLORENCE
AND THE
RENAISSANCE
THE QUATTROCENTO

FLORENCE
AND THE
RENAISSANCE
THE QUATTROCENTO

TEXT BY ALAIN J. LEMAÎTRE

PHOTOGRAPHS BY ERICH LESSING

TERRAIL

Cover illustration

MASOLINO
**The Healing of the Lame and
the Resurrection of Tabitha**
(detail)

Previous page

SANDRO BOTTICELLI
Primavera
(detail)

Opposite

ANDREA DEL VERROCCHIO
David
(detail)

Editors: Jean-Claude Dubost and Jean-François Gonthier
Art director: Bernard Girodroux
English adaptation: Jean-Marie Clarke
Filmsetting: Compo Rive Gauche, Paris

© FINEST S.A. / ÉDITIONS PIERRE TERRAIL, PARIS 1993
ISBN : 2-87939-068-0
Printed in Italy

Table of contents

Opposite

MASACCIO
Adam and Eve Expulsed from the Garden of Eden
(detail)
ca. 1424, fresco, 214 x 90 cm.
Brancacci Chapel, Santa Maria del Carmine, Florence.

A Golden Age

"*T*he most beautiful backdrop is the red sky after sundown. As daylight fades over the Cascine, the Ponte Vecchio–with its ancient houses clustered like so many nests–bars the evening sky like a black ribbon stretched across an expanse of yellow silk. The city spreads all around in harmonies of grey and ocher, while the hills of Fiesole beyond are already shrouded in shades of night. The soft, simple face of San Miniato al Monte glimmers still in the sun's rays, and this last smile never fails to quicken my soul with a quiet, fulfilling grace." In poetic terms such as these did Rainer Maria Rilke describe the magic of Florence at dusk in his *Florentine Diary,* the subtle love song in which he imparted his impressions to Lou Andreas-Salome. His praise went first to the City of Flowers itself–symbolized before a white lily–before touching on its artistic treasures or embarking into aesthetic considerations.

"Florence, however," the young poet added, "does not reveal herself as easily as Venice." To be sure, while the opulent City of the Doges is enlivened twice-over by colorful palazzi and mirroring canals, the charms of Florence are more discreet. The noble dwellings of Venice face outwards, graced with loggias and porticoes, while in Florence only seldom are the massive stone walls pierced with windows, and facades are crowned by severe, often crenellated, cornices.

The city's major architectural landmarks were built during the 14th century, or Trecento. Surrounded by a long wall with no less than 150 bastions, Florence was graced then with two new churches of the mendicant orders–Santa Croce and Santa Maria Novella–the proud and severe fortified Palazzo Vecchio, and the Podesta Palace, or Bargello, all of which were built according to the same principle. In the age of Giotto and Dante, the city still looked to masterpieces of its mature Gothic style like the Loggia dei Lanzi, with its mighty arches and artfully carved pillars, or the market of Or' San Michele and its vast spaces. The cathedral–"the finest and noblest church in Tuscany"–built under the direction of Arnolfo di Cambio, already towered above the rooftops, yet remained without a dome. The men of the Quattrocento were soon to give the superb finishing flourish to this harsh late-medieval townscape.

The new art patrons

Italy at the beginning of the 15th century became ever more involved in the great political transformations of the West. After the dissolution of the Great Schism, the papacy left Avignon once and for all and returned

to the Eternal City, where they undertook a campaign of restoration that gave a major impetus to the Arts. The creation of the Papal States led to a re-focusing of power in the peninsula, giving rise to centers of artistic production that catered to their need for ostentation. To the north and south, communes and republics consolidated their strength and sought a balance through negotiation. In Milan, the Visconti were expelled from their own duchy by the Condottiere Francesco Sforza, while Ferrara rose to cultural prominence under the patronage of such figures as Borso and Lionello d'Este. Naples, after having foiled Rene d'Anjou's attempts to impose his sovereignty, came under the rule of the House of Aragon. Venice in the meantime extended its hegemony to Crete and Cyprus, to the detriment of Siena. The republics of Florence and Siena, seats of the eternally feuding Guelf and Ghibelline factions, exerted their separate influences at the heart of Italy as mercantile and banking powers, while the major families developed artistic patronage along entirely different lines from the princes. It was in this way that the name of Medici became associated with the heyday of Florentine culture. Soldiers of fortune still held sway in military matters and sometimes came to power, which they exercised as they saw fit; either as tyrants, like Malatesta at

SCHOOL OF PIERO DELLA FRANCESCA (LAURANA OR GIULIANO DA SANGALLO?)
The Ideal City
ca. 1460, 60 x 200 cm
Galleria Nazionale delle Marche, Urbino

Rigorously depicted according to the laws of perspective, this is not a view of an existing Italian city, but an architectural fantasy. The perspective techniques developed during the Quattrocento permitted painters and draughtsmen to create balanced and rational linear constructions. Antique architectural elements, such as arches and columns, became an essential part of the artist's pictorial vocabulary and were used here to render an imaginary cityscape. The urbanistic projects of the 16th century derived from this sort of visualization.

Rimini or as enlightened patrons of the arts, like Federigo da Montefeltro, who transformed Urbino into a brilliant court. If the Pazzi rebellion in Volterra ended in a bloody repression, diplomacy had become the rule in the conduct of the affairs of state.

Antiquity, a constant source

While rivalry between the various city states left Dante's dream of a unified Italy unfulfilled, artists and intellectuals found in the Roman genius a common humanist ideal to which they could turn. The Trecento had already been acutely aware of this common past, and considered the monuments of Roman antiquity as symbols of a golden age. For the Quattrocento however, these prestigious remains came to be valued for their own sake. Artists, poets, scholars and statesmen became avid collectors of antique works. The great art-lover Niccolo Niccoli was an intimate of Florentine sculptors and architects like Brunelleschi, Donatello and Lucca della Robbia. He was among those who advised Ghiberti when he set down the first sketches for the famous Baptistery door known as the Gate of Paradise. So lively was the curiosity for all things antique that the Commune of Siena commissioned the sculptor Jacopo della Quercia to portray its Roman ancestry and virtues in the Gaia Fountain. A decisive role was played by the study of antique forms, precise drawings of monuments, and epigraphic transcriptions. Notes and sketches by travellers made the rounds of the studios and workshops, inspiring the talents of painters and sculptors as well as medalists and decorators.

It was here that Florence first manifested its originality. While the courts of Verona, Mantua and Ferrara revelled in the lore of chivalry and the charms of courtly poetry, as imported from Flanders by Van Eyck, Florence and its reformers asserted a diametrically opposed aesthetic. This artistic renewal, aptly termed Renaissance, was paralleled by an intellectual renewal which made the 15th century a fertile era for theoretical speculation. Leon Battista Alberti formulated his thought in fundamental treatises on painting and sculpture before tackling one on architecture; Ghiberti published his *Commentary*, and Piero della Francesca set down his ideas in a *Treatise on Perspective*.

Assimilating the knowledge of the past, artists became theoreticians and elaborated a discipline to rival the antiquated "liberal arts." It was in this light that Alberti appeared to his friend Cristoforo Landino: "How to categorize Alberti? Among what type of scholar does he

belong? Probably the physicists, for he was destined to probe the secrets of nature. Yet there was not a single branch of the mathematical sciences of which he had no knowledge. He was a geometer, arithmetician, astronomer, musician, and the most outstanding specialist of perspective in centuries. His command of all of these disciplines is manifest in the nine books on architecture which flowed from his divine pen.... He wrote a treatise on painting, as well as one on sculpture which he titled *De Statua*. He was not content merely to expound on the arts, he also practiced them. I happen to have in my collections a number of precious works from his chisel and burin, as well as metal casts." Florence provided the most favorable medium for this powerful fusion of the arts and sciences. It was in the workshop of Andrea del Verrocchio that Leonardo da Vinci learned the lessons which he was to apply in Milan with the collaboration of Bramante, the mathematician Luca Pacioli, and Lombardian engineers.

The union of art and science

Training in these disciplines began at an early age. In Florence, as in most other major cities of the peninsula, children sent to lay schools first learned the skills of reading and writing, along with the rudiments of commercial correspondence and basic notarial forms.

At the age of eleven, they were introduced to the Fables of Aesop and the works of Dante but not without being served healthy doses of mathematics–for business purposes mainly. In an age of non-standard shipping units, one had to be able to calculate contents and quantities of shipments fairly rapidly. In fifteenth-century Germany, where norms and measures were established in advance, these calculations were left up to specialists. This was not the case in Quattrocento Italy, hence the constant recourse to geometry. Not surprisingly, a painter like Piero della Francesca wrote a Treatise on Geometry intended for merchants in which he gave indications on how to gauge barrels of goods. Like so many other artists of his time who were trained in mathematics, Piero applied to his forms the same mental operations as merchants to estimate the volume of a container. This taste for geometry, an integral part of the 15th-century art lover's pictorial delectation, was catered to by painters through the representation of objects and elements familiar to students of this discipline: columns, brick towers, fountains of circular or parallelepiped design, tile patterns, etc. In the same way that a painter could reduce the human form or settings to a play of geometrical figures, so could the merchant simplify

all things to geometrical configurations. Piero della Francesca and Paolo Uccello regularly used such devices to catch the eye of the beholder.

The mathematics taught for business purposes in Florence were not limited to geometry either: another branch was arithmetic, the principal application of which was the study of proportions. The rule of 3, also called the Golden Rule or the Merchant's Key was widely used in everyday life to determine ratios whether in currency exchange or to solve the problems posed by the various system of weights and measures practiced in different cities. It was a tool used both by painters and merchants–the one for pictorial applications and the other for commercial transactions. It was precisely this emphasis given in education to techniques of measurement–and thus to geometric concepts–that permitted the men of the Quattrocento to approach works of art, particularly paintings, with a specific attention to formal structures, enabling them to see bodies in terms of volume and surface. The prominence given to mathematics in Renaissance society encouraged painters to make a more or less conspicuous display of their skills in this area, and therefore to satisfy the expectations of the beholder.

While artists subjected the traditional representation of the world to critical examination, medieval scholasticism gave way to objective knowledge gained through direct experience and observation. Considered as a more accurate perception of this, the naturalism and realism that had already been a feature of 14th-century illuminations was systematically developed. Nature and Man, so clearly represented by the masters of Antiquity became the object of a scientific approach.

This new attitude drove artists to modify conventional ideas about observational knowledge. Henceforth the surrounding world was to be represented as it appeared to the eye. To this end, a new basis to pictorial composition was given through the invention of linear perspective, a system according to which vision was organized along straight lines, such that parallel lines running in the same direction in space seem to converge at a single point on the horizon. The challenge to the painter was to apply these principles to create illusionistic space and effects without succumbing to a systematic or arbitrary formalism. Depth was suggested by depicting the progressive decrease in the size of objects and figures as their distance from the observer increases–an illusion which in painting becomes truth.

17

The joys of creation

The new commitment to the arts, no less than pure aesthetic delectation, gave a new impetus to pictorial creation. The major art works of the Quattrocento, especially the great masterpieces of painting, were all commissioned by patrons. In every case, whether for a sacred or a profane picture, an iconographic program for a church or a donor's altarpiece, a major project for a court or a commune, the role played by the patron was a decisive one.

The Florentine merchant Giovanni Rucellai called upon the likes of Filippo Lippi, Verrocchio, Pollaiuolo, and Uccello, as well as masters throughout Italy, to decorate his palace with their works. Concerned not only with enriching his personal collection, Rucellai spent considerable sums on the construction and decoration of churches, an investment which brought him "the utmost pleasure and contentment, for it served to glorify God, honor the city, and preserve my memory. Commissioning an altarpiece for a church or a fresco for a chapel fulfilled all the needs of a patron: his taste for art, his civic image, his piety, and–last but not least his desire for immortality.

The art patron influenced painters, sculptors and architects alike through his financial commitment

and through the destination of his commission. Only Madonna figures and pieces of furniture (like the marriage *cassoni* mass-produced by minor artists or established studios when business was slow) were exempt from the all-powerful patron. The production of works of art was treated like any other commercial transaction, and subject as such, to contractual obligations agreed upon by both parties. A contract was drawn up stipulating the terms of the commission, which ranged from the most general considerations–like the entire content of an iconographic program, as in the case of Ghiberti's door for the Baptistery or of the decoration of the Medici Palace in Florence–down to the most particular, such as the size of the work, types of figures, or pigments and time spent by the artist. In 1457, Filippo Lippi at work on a triptych for Giovanni di Cosimo de' Medici, wrote to his client for more funds in order to finish his work under the best conditions: "I have scrupulously respected your instructions concerning the picture and taken great care with each detail. The figure of St. Nichael is so close to completion that I have gone to see Bartolomeo Martelli, for his armor and other clothing are all to be painted in gold and silver. Martelli told me to do exactly as you wished." Because of the richness of the ornamentation, Lippi requested an extra sixty florins, all the while promising to finish the painting within the next forty days.

MASTER OF THE ADIMARI CASSONE
The Adimari Cassone (detail of a panel)
ca. 1440,
Galleria dell'Accademia,
Florence

Produced in large numbers during the 14th and 15th centuries, cassoni, or marriage coffers, gave artists the opportunity to depict festive and colorful ceremonies in settings based on Florentine monuments. Depicted here is the Adimari-Ricasoli wedding feast held on the Piazza San Giovanni.

Above and opposite (detail)

PAOLO UCCELLO
**Scene from the Life of
Noah–the Flood and
Recession of the Water**
ca. 1446-1448, fresco touched
up with tempera, mounted on
canvas,
215 x 520 cm.
Chiostro Verde, Santa Maria
Novella, Florence.

The mazzocchio *was a Florentine
headpiece made of wood or reeds
which was used as a base for tall
bonnets draped with scarves. It was a
favorite accessory of Paolo Uccello
and other Tuscan painters, like Piero
della Francesca, because it lent itself
so well to geometric and perspective
construction. In this detail of* The
Flood, *it hangs oddly around this
figure's neck and may have a
symbolic meaning (life-saving ring?).*

The patron could therefore have a very precise idea of the work to be made by the artist, and he was often in direct contact with the painters and sculptors in question. Contracts drawn up in Florence at the beginning of the Quattrocento called for high grades of pigment to be used in painting, especially where ultramarine-blue was concerned. The best quality, made of lapis-lazuli imported from the Orient, was quite expensive but of greater intensity and stability than the corresponding German pigment made of bicarbonate of copper. This bright blue was used to highlight a figure, gesture, scene or important object, and in the contracts its grade–and nuance–was often stipulated in terms of florins per ounce.

As the 15th century progressed however, precious materials like gold and ultramarine blue became less and less important for the Florentine masters. Gold, a focus of attention in pictures at the beginning of the century, receded in importance until it became relegated to the frame alone. Rich pigments like ultramarine blue were also less and less in demand among patrons. This regression of gold and precious materials in painting marked a turning point in the practice of this art and in habits of ostentation. Attention was diverted from the flashy effect of materials and turned ever more toward the artist's ability. Leon Battista Alberti denounced the systematic use of gold in painting, praising instead the workmanship of the talented painter who had "depicted the shimmering of gold with ordinary pigments alone" in Virgil's *Dido*. As ultramarine blue and gold backgrounds fell out of favor and were replaced by actual landscapes, art patrons sought artists who were skilled in painting hills, fields, castles, cities, rivers and birds of all kinds. Contracts specified the parts to be treated respectively by master and assistant, for skill was the prime commodity paid for. Whether a prince or a merchant, the Quattrocento patron of the arts displayed his wealth by paying for great talent, to the detriment of gold and expensive materials, even though only a handful of artists and connoisseurs were in a position to judge the relative merits of each through their works. Towards the end of the 15th century, while on the lookout for artists to decorate the Certosa of Pavia, the Duke of Milan received a report from his agent in Florence on four of the most brilliant stars in painting: Botticelli, Filippino Lippi, Perugino and Ghirlandaio. He singled out Sandro Botticelli for his ability to paint both "on walls and panels," noted the quality of his technique and his unerring sense of proportion. Filippino Lippi offered a gentler handling than his master, yet not more in the way of ability. Perugino he called "an outstanding

master, especially on walls." In Domenico Ghirlandaio who was equally skilled in fresco and panel painting, he praised his capacity for work. All had worked for Lorenzo il Magnifico and he was "hard put to choose the best." Patrons thus played artists against each other, including top masters, judging them for their qualities in painting frescoes and panels, as well as their respective manners.

Most of the works which mark the pictorial and architectural history of the Quattrocento are of a religious nature. Many churches were built at the initiative of lay donors; Florence owes the churches of San Lorenzo and San Marco, the Badia, and the novitiate of Santa Croce to Cosimo de' Medici. Nobles had more modest chapels or oratories built, like Santa Maria degli Angioli or the Pazzi Chapel. The Brancacci Chapel where Masaccio executed frescoes, or those in Arezzo, where Piero della Francesca painted the *Legend of the True Cross*, have a similar origin.

The pictures themselves had a specific function as images in the strict ecclesiastical scheme of things: to give religious instruction to those who could not read; to put the sacred mysteries into a striking and memorable form; to inspire devotion in the beholder. The Church was of course vulnerable to whatever liberties the artists might take in their interpretation. The Bishop of Florence St. Antoninus' strictures against unorthodox representations were of no avail; art constantly overstepped the bounds of theology. In his own cathedral, the faithful could see the apocryphal subject of *Saint Thomas and the Virgin's Girdle* carved on the Porta della Mandorla. Gentile da Fabriano, on a commission for the merchant Palla Strozzi from 1423, painted an *Adoration of the Magi* which displayed not only the fashionably attired figures so decried by the bishop, but also dogs and monkeys, considered to be conducive to "day-dreaming and idle thoughts." Even so, Florence and Tuscany in the Quattrocento were exempt from the kind of idolatry current in Germany then.

The painter's task was therefore to visualize the various episodes of the Christian epic for a public that was itself trained in spiritual exercises of this kind. Sermons formed the starting point for pictorial representation. The painter had at his disposal a veritable repertoire of imagery that followed emotional categories precisely established by the preacher. It may rightly be said that Quattrocento painting developed within the framework of these categories more often than not, even if it occasionally lapsed into the profane.

Opposite and above (detail)

FRA ANGELICO
Annunciation, Adoration of the Magi, and Virgin and Child with Ten Saints
1434, tempera on wood
84 x 50
Museo de San Marco, Florence

During the course of the Quattrocento the taste for gold and precious materials declined in favor of a growing appreciation of the skill of the painters. Fra Angelico used gold early in his career then abandoned it, often replacing it with landscape backgrounds.

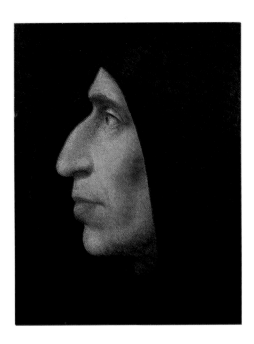

Above

BARTOLOMEO DELLA PORTA
Savonarola
1497
Museo de San Marco, Florence

*Linked to Savonarola, the painter
left us a striking portrait of the
controversial preacher in profile view,
a fashion of the late 15th century.
Condemning the luxury and
corruption of the Medici no less than
the philosophy of the humanists, the
Prior of San Marco achieved much
success through his simplicity and
power of conviction, qualities that are
visible in this likeness.*

Opposite

FILIPPINO LIPPI
**Saint Peter's Dispute with
Simon the Magician, and the
Martyrdom of Saint Peter**
(detail showing presumed
portrait of Botticelli ca. 1484,
fresco, 232 x 588 cm.
Brancacci Chapel, Santa Maria
del Carmine, Florence.

*In the middle of the fresco illustrating
two episodes from the end of the
saint's life, Filippino Lippi included
a portrait (presumed) of his master
among a group of bystanders. The
Quattrocento raised the status of the
artists and brought them to a new
awareness of their role in society and
history.*

The artists of the 15th century who often organized themselves into common workshops, benefitted from the high esteem of their patrons and from a certain corporate pride.

All were enthusiastically conscious of living in a great period of artistic creation, a sentiment to which Alberti gave expression in dedicating his Treatise on Painting to Brunelleschi in the following terms: "Ever since returning to my homeland–by far the most beautiful of all lands–from the long exile to which my family was condemned, I have seen many works–yours above all, Filippo, then those of our dear friend the sculptor Donato, those of Nencio, Luca, and Masaccio, which are as praiseworthy and full of skill as the most famous and venerable works of antiquity. I realized then that if we have any virtues worthy of praise, we owe them more to our own diligence and intelligence, than to the legacy of nature or our time. It was no doubt simpler for the ancients to achieve supremacy in the arts, for they had guidelines and models to imitate, while we must attain this knowledge through our own efforts alone. So much the greater, I dare say, will be our glory, for, without guides and models, we have created arts and sciences never before seen or heard of."

SANDRO BOTTICELLI
The Adoration of the Magi
(detail)
1475, tempera on wood,
111 x l34 cm.
Galleria degli Uffizi, Florence.

Art patronage played a significant role in the history of Quattrocento painting: all of the major works were commissions. The theme of the Epiphany was especially popular among patrons, for it showed the devotion of the powerful to the humbly-born Jesus. In this work, Botticelli turned the Adoration of the Magi into an apotheosis of the Medici and their entourage.

SANDRO BOTTICELLI
The Adoration of the Magi
(detail with self-portrait)

*Botticelli self-consciously included his own
likeness in a depiction which has more to do with
contemporary politics than with religious history.*

Masaccio:
A New Way
of Painting

Above

MASACCIO
**Adam and Eve expelled from
the Garden of Eden**
1424 (?), fresco, 214 x 90 cm.
Brancacci Chapel, Santa Maria
del Carmine, Florence.

Opposite

MASACCIO
**The Distribution of Alms and
The Punishment of Ananias**
(detail of woman and child)
1426-1427 (?), fresco,
232 x 157 cm.
Brancacci Chapel, Santa Maria
del Carmine, Florence.

*A*t the beginning of the 15th century, Gothic painting characterized by imaginary landscapes, graceful figures and gold or floral backgrounds–was perfectly at home in Siena, where painters like Stefano di Giovanni and Sassetta continued the tradition of precious devotional images. Florence, on the other hand, was won over to the Renaissance style through the efforts of Brunelleschi, Ghiberti and Donatello, among other initiators listed by Alberti in his *Treatise on Painting*. The only painter that he mentions–Masaccio–was to mark, in the brief ten years of his career, the history of the Quattrocento as a whole. With Masaccio, the detailed manner of painting derived from manuscript illumination, with its elegant corteges of splendidly attired figures, became a thing of the past. He painted instead arid landscapes, solemn processions and simple drapery, portraying faces expressive not of visionary inspiration, but of plain realism.

Nature as model

Nothing is known of Masaccio's childhood and training except that he was born in 1401 in Castel San Giovanni in Altura (between Florence and Arezzo) with the name Tommaso di Ser Giovanni di Mone Cassai. He is

31

first mentioned in Florence in 1422 as a member of the Guild of Physicians and Apothecaries. From Masolina da Panica he learned only the craft of painting, then, with no other known master and with only Giotto's frescoes at Santa Croce as models, he dropped the Gothic idiom in favor of a new sense of volume and space. His "reformulation" of Giotto was sustained by Brunelleschi and Donatello's experiments with perspective. Masaccio in fact, soon moved away from the studio system to work free-lance on projects in Florence, where he could learn from the innovators themselves.

The major figures of the Italian Renaissance, adapting to the new conditions of the market, sought equally novel forms of work organization. Around 1424, Masaccio and Masolino da Panicale joined forces in an association similar to Donatello and Michelozzo's "company," whereby two artists collaborated on a temporary basis on the same commission, dividing the labor along rational lines and without giving up their individuality. The two painters thus worked together on *St. Ann, the Virgin and Child with Angels* for the Uffizi, then around 1425-1431 on frescoes for the Branda Chapel in Rome and the altarpiece for Santa Maria Maggiore. Masaccio seems to have worked alone on the fresco of the *Holy Trinity* for Santa Maria Novella around 1427, but he collaborated with Masolino on the frescoes for the Branaccio Chapel at the Carmine in Florence between 1423 and 1428, the date of the former's death. A friend of Brunelleschi and protege of Donatello, Masaccio was known for his feeling for volume, the intelligence of his compositions, and his mastery of perspective, qualities in which he outshone Masolino. The works of the two may well be on the walls of the same chapels, at times to the point of being indistinguishable, but only Masaccio served as a model for the future. According to Vasari, all of the most famous painters and sculptors went to study them. Leonardo da Vinci himself expressed his admiration in these terms: "By the perfection of his pictorial works, he proved that all those who do not take nature as the model for their art labor in vain." Masaccio's career was all too brief, but the few monumental frescos that he left behind, nourished by Donatello's influence and Brunelleschi's concern for perspective, suffice to assert his genius and ensure his fame.

An artistic landmark: the Brancacci Chapel

Masaccio's talent is readily apparent in the chapel which Felice Brancacci commissioned from Masolino around 1424. Already, in decorating the entrance arch with *The Expulsion of Adam and Eve from Paradise*,

Masaccio departed from the tradition of depicting a frame, a holdover from Medieval illuminations. Nor is there any gilding or plethora of details. While Masolino, in his *Temptation of Adam and Eve*, took great pains in painting the Tree and its foliage, Masaccio represented a barren and inhospitable landscape. The gate of Eden, like its former tenants, has been reduced to the bare essentials. The archangel looming above with his sword does not detract one's attention from the main protagonists of the episode, taking their first steps into a cold, cruel world. Adam, the last to leave, succumbs to grief and buries his face in his hands; Eve cries out in despair and makes the classic gesture of modesty. United by a common impulsion, the first two mortals walk forth, the one withdrawing in shame, the other bursting with anguish and sorrow. There are evident references to Antiquity: Masaccio borrowed Eve's pose from Hellenistic figures of the Venus Pudica type, while he may have drawn on the Apollo Belvedere for Adam's torso. The nudes are treated in a realistic manner, and for the first time in Renaissance painting the human figure is a living body. Compared to Masolino's figures on the opposite wall, frozen in the courtly gestures and attitudes of Gothic iconography, Masaccio's figures have a dramatic presence which constitutes a radical break from the medieval forms which were still fashionable in Tuscany.

In *The Tribute Money*, the most famous scene in the Brancacci Chapel, Masaccio's art reached a peak in the handling of volume and space, line and relief, color and light. The three parts of the incident, as related in the Gospel of Matthew (17: 24-27), have been brought together in the same pictorial space. In the middle, the question of the tribute is being put and Jesus' disciples anxiously await his answer. On the left, Peter is shown recovering the piece of money as instructed, while on the right he gives it to the tax-collector. The scene is set on a hilly landscape depicted with effects of atmospheric and linear perspective such as Paolo Uccello was later to take up in his own works: progressive change of tonal values and size of objects according to distance. The apostles are huddled around Christ in a tight group, seemingly aware of the significance of what is happening before their eyes. The expressive faces and gazes, the solemn bearing and simple drapery, reminiscent of Greek philosophers, all point to Masaccio's new classical sources. The artist also demonstrated his knowledge of perspective: to the spectator standing in the chapel—behind the tax-collector—pictorial space and real space seem to be continuous. The oblique lines of the tax-collector's house, which Masaccio placed on the right, direct the gaze into the composition, while a procession of rhythmic elements

Above

MASACCIO
The Tribute Money
(detail showing Peter giving the tribute to the tax collector in front of the house in Capernaum)

Opposite

The Tribute Money
(detail with apostles)
The figures depicted in The Tribute Money *are grouped in an elliptical configuration, a classical formal device already used in Early Christian art.*

such as recessing mountains, hedges, and clouds in a softly graded sky, pulls it into depth.

The same sources and effects may be seen in the fresco of *The Baptism*, an episode recounted in the Acts of the Apostles (2:41), which precedes *The Distribution of Alms* and *The Punishment of Ananias* in the Brancacci Chapel cycle. As in the *Tribute Money* the aspiring converts form a circular group while seeming to extend into the valley like a procession. The kneeling figure receiving baptism is straight out of the standard Christian iconography, but the robust nude and Apollonian beauty of the young man points toward Greco-Roman statuary. In the *Distribution of Alms* and *Cripple healed by St. Peter's shadow*, Masaccio depicted the scenes in an urban setting which he described in some detail, from the stonework of a palace to the classical elements of a church facade at the end of the street. Freeing himself from bookish principles and from the conventional repertory of forms and figures then in vogue, Masaccio's originality manifested itself in an intense expressivity and brought a new dimension to realism. To quote Pierre Francastel: "From then on, man was to be defined no longer by the deeds and documents that positioned him historically, but by the immediate sensory and physical facts which create presence."

The Brancacci Chapel is imbued with the spirit of the Quattrocento. Masaccio's frescoes were a complement to those of Masolino; then, in 1481-1482, Filippino Lippi completed the cycle left unfinished by his illustrious predecessors at their death. There is no point in trying to reduce Masolino's and Masaccio's works to an antagonistic face-off. The relationship between their respective scenes on the walls is so balanced that, in all likelihood, the two painters worked according to a single concept. The iconographic program represented exalts the role played by the apostle Peter and the Church he founded. The overall unity of conception in no way prevented the artists from expressing themselves each in their own idiom; yet the clarity of the color-schemes and compositions create a continuous optical experience before executing the *Tribute Money* and the *Resurrection of Tabitha*, Masaccio and Masolino together thought out the perspective scheme and staging of the two frescoes. Their differences are in manner alone. While Masaccio used broad brush strokes to render the faces, undulating hair, and ample torsos, Masolino painted on a more moderate scale, working in small brush strokes to build up more subtly graded volumes. The robust figures of the first are counterbalanced by the gentler forms of the latter.

It was Masaccio's realism that appealed to his contemporaries, and his influence spanned the century

FILIPPINO LIPPI
Saint Peter's Dispute with Simon the Magician and The Martyrdom of Saint Peter
(detail with crucifixion)
Brancacci Chapel, Santa Maria del Carmine, Florence.

Opposite

MASACCIO
The Distribution of Alms and The Punishment of Ananias
1425-1427 (?), fresco, 232 x 157 cm.
Brancacci Chapel, Santa Maria del Carmine, Florence.

until it crossed the path of Filippino Lippi, who finished the decoration of the Brancacci Chapel by depicting scenes from the story of Peter as told in the Golden Legend. Picking up where Masaccio had left off, he painted the *Resurrection of the Son of Theophilus* and *Saint Peter on a Throne* completing the other scenes without taking into account the modular relationship which the two masters had established between the frescoes. Lippi strove to recapture the realism and rhythm of Masaccio and Masolino, but his overall sense of balance and perspective proved to be unequal to the task.

Reacting against the facile elegance of the Gothic, Masaccio based his work on volume, space and light. The Brancacci Chapel became a necessary stepping stone for the artists of the Quattrocento, but Florentine painting was host to a variety of pictorial languages, as the work of Fra Angelico made so splendidly clear.

FILIPPINO LIPPI
Saint Peter freed from Prison
1484, fresco, 232 x .89 cm.
Brancacci Chapel, Santa Maria
del Carmine, Florence.

*Awakened by an angel, Saint Peter
is led out of his prison cell past a
sleeping guard.*

Opposite

MASACCIO
**Saint Peter Healing the Lamb
with His Shadow**
1425-1427 (?), fresco
232 x 162 cm.
Brancacci Chapel, Santa Maria
del Carmine, Florence.

*To illustrate this episode from the
Acts of the Apostles, Masaccio
depicted not squalid surroundings,
but a splendid classical city with
majestic monuments. The street,
composed in perspective, is lined with
Florentine houses, including a palace
with stone facing reminiscent of the
Palazzo Vecchio or Palazzo Pitti. It
leads to a church and bell-tower built
according to the ideas of Alberti.*

MASACCIO AND FILIPPINO LIPPI
**The Resurrection of the Son
of Theophilus and Saint Peter
on a Throne** (details)
1428 (?), fresco, 232 x 597 cm.
Brancacci Chapel, Santa Maria
del Carmine, Florence.

*Masaccio and Filippino Lippi
depicted the miracle made by Peter
after his liberation from prison as it is
told in the Golden Legend.
Masaccio introduced contemporary
figures unrelated to the biblical event,
including a group in which he
portrayed himself and fellow artists:
from right to left, Brunelleschi in a
black hood, Masolino da Panicale,
Masaccio himself, and Leon Battista
Alberti.
Filippino Lippi executed the figure of
the son of Theophilus.*

Fra Angelico
and
Light

Guido di Pietro was born along
with the Quattrocento in a village of the Mugello region, to
the northeast of Florence, and was apprenticed at an early age
to a Florentine master. By 1417 he was already registered as a
painter in the St. Nicolas company at the Carmine. Contrary
to what tradition might suggest, the man who came to be
called Fra Angelico started out as an artist, then became a
monk, and not the other way around. We find his name
profanely mentioned again on a payroll in connection with
the decoration of San Stefano al Ponte in 1418.

The student of Lorenzo Monaco

Around this time the peasant-born
painter took his vows at the Dominican monastery in Fiesole.
In this reformed order of preaching friars he came into
contact with the discipline of its founder and the thinking of
St. Thomas Aquinas. In this austere environment faithful to
the asceticism of the early Christians, Fra Giovanni, as he was
then called, was blessed with the friendship of the prior
Antoninus, future bishop of Florence and saint. It was
probably there as well that he met Piero di Giovanni—a
Camaldulan monk who had already made a name for himself
as the painter Lorenzo Monaco—and became his student.

Above and opposite (detail)

Fra Angelico
The Last Judgement (detail of
Paradise)
ca. 1430-1433, tempera on
wood,
105 x 210 cm.
Museo di San Marco, Florence.

*Painted for the Camaldulan convent
of Santa Maria degli Angioli, Fra
Angelico's* Last Judgement *is still
in the spirit of the work of Lorenzo
Monaco. For one last time he
represented the Gothic world of grace,
using the sparkle of gold and
shimmering colors to create a divine
feast. The treatment of space,
however, obeys the rules of
perspective and thus places Fra
Angelico squarely in the
Quattrocento.*

49

At the scriptorium of Santa Maria di Angioli in Florence, this master had found the perfect environment for the development of his talent. The fullness and definition of his forms is in the tradition of Andrea Orcagna, but the lyricism of his colors and his sensitivity to linear rhythms owes everything to Sienese painting. Starting from Tuscan illuminations, Lorenzo Monaco developed a style that combined all of the aesthetic tendencies of the nascent Quattrocento; in compositions of unassuming simplicity, a dreamy mysticism and grace cohabitate with the refinement of the International Gothic. His figures bathe in a contrast of unreal light which accentuates their elongation and sway. This development is visible in his miniature work no less than in his altarpieces: consider the grandiose panel of the *Coronation of the Virgin* painted in 1413 for the cloister of Santa Maria degli Angioli, or better yet, the *Adoration of the Magi* most likely painted for the church of San Egidio in Florence. In this last work, the poetic and mystic sensitivity revealed in Lorenzo Monaco's miniatures found its most perfect expression. In depicting this sacred event, he used every artistic means at his disposal, contrasting the serenity of the Virgin, the contemplation of the kings, and the excitement of the witnesses clustered behind them in this imaginary landscape.

From his master, Fra Giovanni da Fiesole, one can say that he kept the Gothic atmosphere, gentle brushwork, and subtle harmonies of predominantly light colors.

The frescoes for San Marco's

Fra Giovanni was probably ordained between 1427 and 1429. Several years later, the Dominican monks of Fiesole relocated to the convent of San Marco in Florence, recently reconstructed thanks to Medici patronage, by the architect who built their palace, Michelozzo. While Cosimo de' Medici, lord and master of Florence, enriched the convent with his collection of rare Greek and Byzantine manuscripts, Fra Giovanni and his assistants began, in 1436, to decorate the walls of the monks' cells with a remarkable series of frescoes which brought not only inspiration to the friars but also enduring fame to their creator. The myth of the blessed Fra Giovanni was already in the making. Although venerated during his own lifetime, he was never to be granted beatification by the Church. The epithet "Angelico"–the Angelic–was given to him by the humanist Cristoforo Landino and ratified by popular consent. In 1449, he turned down the Pope's offer to make him archbishop of Florence,

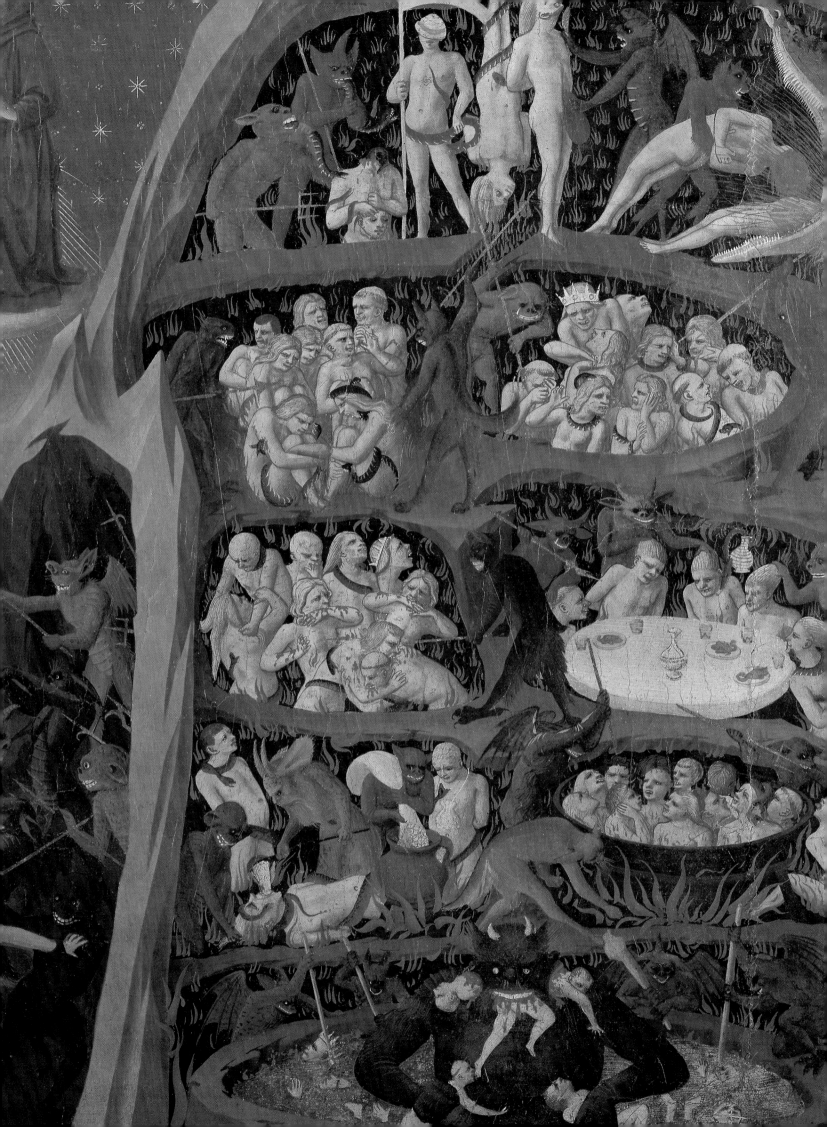

Above and opposite (detail)

FRA ANGELICO
The Descent from the Cross
(detail with Mary Magdalene)
ca. 1430-1433, tempera on
wood,
176 x 185 cm.
Museo de San Marco, Florence

*Lorenzo Monaco executed the
pediment and predella panels of this*
Descent from the Cross *which
was originally intended for the
sacristy of Santa Trinità. The
contribution of other collaborators is
not unlikely but the figure of Christ
is the work of Fra Angelico alone.*

Left and opposite

FRA ANGELICO
The Descent from the Cross
(details)

Like the image of Christ, the figures of Fra Angelico have a sculptural serenity inherited from the art of Masaccio. The figure on the ladder with a black hat has been given the likeness of Michelozzo, the architect who rebuilt the monastery of San Marco.

preferring instead to become prior of the Fiesole convent in the following year. His life was an itinerant one nonetheless, with commissions calling him to Orvieto in 1447 to paint frescoes on the ceiling of a chapel in the cathedral, then back to Florence, to Prato, and on to Rome, where he worked at the basilica of St. Peter's, the new palace of Nicolas V, and the Pope's Sudiolo until his death in 1455.

The period which saw the walls of San Marco being covered with mystical frescoes was a special time indeed in the history of the Church. The Council of Constance put an end to the papal schism in 1419, and Rome and Byzantium became the two poles of a restored Christendom which basked in the light of a new humanism. Fra Angelico and his fellow friars worked in re-invigorated atmosphere: for the venerated monk art was a religious vocation and he was its instrument, giving form to teachings and focus to meditation in the solitary cells.

The Orvieto chronicles, written during Fra Angelico's lifetime, describe him as a "wonderful friar, lord of painting, whose fame exceeds that of all other painters in Italy." Vasari said of him that he never reworked his paintings and that he would paint crucifixes with "tears streaming down his face." Contemplating the works of Fra Angelico, Michelangelo later remarked: "It must be that this worthy monk visited in Heaven, and that he was allowed to choose his models there."

Fra Angelico's work, marked by different currents and an evolution from the Gothic towards the Florentine Renaissance is difficult to define. In his early years he was influenced by the miniature: the reliquaries of Santa Maria Novella, with their modelling and guilloche decors, and the *Coronation of the Virgin* at the convent in Fiesole, with its massed groups of figures, are all related to the art of illumination. His debt to Lorenzo Monaco is, on the other hand, more clearly visible in the elasticity of his figures, his choice of color and brilliant gold backgrounds. Painted around 1430 for the convent of Santa Maria degli Angioli, his *Last Judgement*, with its shimmering colors and gold, proclaim him as a follower of Lorenzo. The sharpness of his forms and his taste for arabesque however, show his affinity with Sienese painting and with Simone Martini in particular. He was not indifferent to the art of Ghiberti, with whom he collaborated in 1433 to execute the *Madonna dei Linaiuoli* (linen merchants). He was also familiar with Brunelleschi, Donatello and Masaccio, and integrated their lessons in his depiction of architectural settings and modelling of volumes, all the while elaborating his own pictorial idiom.

Above and opposite

FRA ANGELICO
The Descent from the Cross
(details)

Despite a certain Gothic nostalgia, particularly apparent in the group of women, the Descent from the Cross *belongs to the Renaissance. Traditional piety and spirituality are combined with the austerity of the humanists and a quest for scientific naturalism.*

To make his altarpieces, Fra Angelico worked according to two basic models as requested by his patrons. The first was the polyptych, often used by the Primitives, which consisted of a number of separate panels with Gothic frames, each containing a single figure within its polychrome or gilt confines, as in Perugia or Cortona. The second type, called *Sacra Conversazione*, brought the figures together into a single panel and became a major theme of the Renaissance. It shows the Virgin set off against a typical decor, surrounded by saints with precisely-assigned positions. In his art, Fra Angelico struck a balance between the forms of the Primitives and Quattrocento modernism.

He integrated pictorial innovations into his works in a variety of ways. The influence of Antiquity is most readily apparent in his architectural settings. In a panel of the predella of the *Madonna dei Linaiuoli*, he depicted a loggia and wall with Ionic pilasters to frame the *Martyrdom of St. Mark*. The Christ Child in the San Marco *Sacra Conversazione* is dressed in an antique-style costume. Yet, though Antiquity is omnipresent in his frescoes for the chapel of Nicolas V at the Vatican, he cast architecture in a representational, rather than structural role.

Fra Angelico's use of linear perspective was anything but systematic. He was among the first to use a receding, step-wise arrangement for the attendant crowd of faithful in his *Coronation of the Virgin*, but he retained the curved apsidal formation in other compositions. The secondary elements were in any case only a means to situate the main event. In the *Annunciation* he painted for San Marco, Fra Angelico displayed his mastery of perspective by giving a realistic depiction of the cloister in which the scene takes place. It is evident however, that the representation of an illusionistic space was not his major concern. The outstanding feature of this fresco is the sense of presence in these figures: the Virgin sits virtually motionless before the angel locked in a hieratic pose, in the middle of a plain whitewashed cell furnished only with a stool. As with Gabriel and the Virgin in the *Annunciation*, or the Three Kings and their cortege in the San Marco *Adoration*, Fra Angelico sought above all to bring out the relationship between the main characters.

This is not to say that compositional considerations were of any less importance. He rendered the walls of Jerusalem with consummate mastery in the San Marco *Deposition*, and the cubic citadel which looms above them is a strict application of Renaissance geometry. The disposition of rectilinear elements like trees, both to divert the eye and contribute to spatial definition, demonstrate a particularly

INRI

alue mundi salutare · salue salue iesu chare · Cruci tue me ascare · factum uere tu scis quare · Presta mihi copiam

SALVE MATER... VIRGINIS INTACTE CVM VENERIS ANTE FIGVRAM PRETEREVNDO CAVE NE SILEATVR AVE

strong concern for rhythm which anticipates the work of Piero della Francesca.

When he was not using the techniques of linear perspective to create a sense of depth, he explored the resources of color and light, playing on tonal contrasts by alternating light and dark planes. Fra Angelico was no chiaroscurist however: he built his volumes up progressively through increasing concentrations of pigment, and succeeded in creating light through color alone. As a devout follower of the teachings of St. Thomas Aquinas, he also assimilated his theory of colors. As a result, his colors emerge from and fade into the immaterial, and light radiates from his diaphanous tonalities. His complete mastery of tints is nowhere more apparent than in his *Coronation of the Virgin*, in which Christ, draped in white in the midst of a light-filled celestial sphere, crowns a radiantly white Virgin. Only towards the end of his life did Fra Angelico begin to apply his colors more freely, using saturated hues.

Painting and preaching

The painting that culminated in the frescoes of San Marco was an inseparable adjunct to the pastoral mission. In the first phase of his career, Fra Angelico put his art at the service of the Dominican message, using images to teach the untutored faithful that they were to worship. The painter used extreme accents of color, like blue and red—not to mention gold—as devices to catch the eye. Prominently placed above altars, Polyptychs were designed to please the eye with representations of nature and architecture no less than to focus piety. In the paintings which adorned the churches assembling the worshippers, the divine message was embodied in figures of Gothic grace. The blessed Virgin appeared as a princess in all her finery. Fra Angelico, sensitive to natural detail, gave glimpses of fields and hills in his works. He was in fact the first to depict and authentic Italian landscape, that of Lake Trasimeno. With the eye of a botanist, he chose flowers from the Tuscan countryside and gardens and transposed them into his pictures. In so doing, he was following the example of popular preachers. He was well-versed in the writings of Giovanni Dominici, a Dominican of strict observance who celebrated flowers in his *laudi* to glorify the blessings of the Heavenly realm: "Here is the bloom of the field of fields the gladiolus of the valley of the just, the rose which does not age, the violet which does not wilt, posies and cinnamon and all the fragrances of the Holy Kingdom."

When the doors of the monks' cells at San Marco close, the brightly-colored frescoes disappear. The

images of the natural world suddenly disappear. Of course the paintings remain accessible to the poor, the pilgrims and other visitors, but accessory details have been reduced. The *Crucifixion* in the Chapter Room, used exclusively by members of the Dominican Order, is completely devoid of landscape elements. The frescoes are features of the monk's everyday life, and their message is couched in terms appropriate to the environment. After passing the gate, on the upstairs landing the monks could gaze upon one last fresco with a decor before entering a pictorial realm which Fra Angelico and his assistants designed with a maximal economy of means. Off the corridor, in the cells to which the monks retired for their solitary prayers and meditations devoted to God, the figures on the wall are steeped in a light both natural and supernatural. Here, the Virgin becomes again a humble servant of the Lord. Opposite her, in the bare cell, the Divine Messenger is just an angel, a spiritual creature. The world painted on the walls of the cells is a mystical one, outside of time. The faces of Fra Angelico's figures radiate pure bliss. In the last analysis, the frescoes of San Marco are the creation of a unique vision, that of Fra Angelico, who revealed his key when he said that "to paint the things of Christ, one must live with Christ."

Even if Fra Angelico's work lacks the pictorial discipline which characterizes the other masters of the Quattrocento, even if there is something conventional about certain of his figures, his radiant portrayal of the Christian mystic drama is one of the crowning achievements of the pictorial Renaissance. Rarely have works of art been such fitting transmitters of that spark of intelligence which reveals to man not only the divine mysteries, but also the secret meaning of the things and beings of this world.

By his intimate association of pictorial means and doctrinal message, Fra Angelico may be said to belong to the Byzantine tradition. He was not a narrative painter, the predellas notwithstanding any of his iconographic themes were taken from the Eastern Church, as transmitted to the West by illuminators in manuscripts such as those donated by Cosimo to San Marco. Open to Oriental influences, Fra Angelico was not dazzled by Byzantine opulence, but made the spectacle of color coincide with the revelation of spiritual truth.

Architects
and
the Art of Building

Of all the building projects which were underway in Florence at the beginning of the 15th century, none called on more artists than that of the Cathedral. Despite the decisions taken in 1367, Santa Maria del Fiore was not yet finished. Giotto's campanile, with niches still to be filled and medallions to be carved, was a cause of concern among artists. The Baptistery boasted the bronze door of Andrea Pisano, but the competition which brought Ghiberti to the fore had yet to be launched. Three sculptors—Acopo della Quercia, Nanni di Banco, and the young Donatello—were busy with the door of the Mandorla, on the north transept of the Duomo. The most daunting problem which faced the architects as the dawn of the Quattrocento was at the very heart of the edifice. Begun in 1296 by Arnolfo di Cambio, and after undergoing numerous alterations, the Cathedral one century later reached the level of the cornice of the main nave. The final plan seems to have been established in 1367 by a team of eight architects who decided upon raising a dome over the crossing of the transept and scrapping the previous plans. The octagonal shape of the dome and its span were determined therefore by the progressive labor and experience of the men of the Trecento. The Cathedral however, had yet to find the architect able to raise the dome, spanning over 41 meters at its base, without using external buttresses. The man for the job was a product of the new era: Brunelleschi.

Opposite

FILIPPO BRUNELLESCHI
Exedra, tambour and dome of the Cathedral
1413: completion of the tambour
1420-1426: building of dome.
Diameter: 41 m
Santa Maria del Fiore, Florence.

The impossibility of using a traditional vault construction and the absence of buttresses around the tambour led Brunelleschi to design a ribbed ogival cupola with a double shell.

Brunelleschi–pioneering architect

Filippo Brunelleschi was born in 1377 into a well-established Florentine family. The son of a notary, he benefited early on from a particularly thorough education, for it included all seven of the Liberal Arts. He soon opted for the visual arts. From the day of his admission into the goldsmiths' guild at the age of 21 until his death in 1446, he displayed an insatiable thirst for theoretical knowledge and daring experiments which opened new horizons for the applied arts. Brunelleschi's first contribution to the problem of the Cathedral's dome was not made in his capacity as architect however. From the laying of the cornerstone onward, all the craft guilds were called upon to provide their expertise on a daily basis. The competition organized in 1401 for the Baptistery door–which Brunelleschi lost to his rival Ghiberti–showed the diversity of artists and their origins, and that goldsmiths were involved in all the major projects of the city. In the case of the Duomo, several projects were put forth during 1417-1418, but never taken up. In 1423, Brunelleschi's project for the dome was accepted and he was given full responsibility for the works in 1426. This decision marks an unprecedented departure from medieval corporate practices: a single individual is given recognition for his architectural ideas and entrusted with the direction of every aspect of the construction, down to the ordering of the tools and machines necessary for the undertaking. While medieval builders customarily vaulted cathedrals by raising wooden scaffolding to the desired height with armatures to be covered with masonry, Brunelleschi proposed a radically new solution. First, he designed a dome with two shells, one over the other to reduce the weight of the materials. Then, as support, he used the strong existing internal ribs, extending them upwards to form the projecting arch segments visible on the outside of the eight-sided dome. Lastly, he used specially-designed instruments including a lifting machine. The construction required perfect craftsmanship because the bricks and stone had to be laid in circles, and on the part of the architect, a good deal of abstract reckoning was necessary to arrive at an overall vision; hence a greater reliance on rigorous calculations and geometry than on the empirical tradition of the masons.

These are the reasons why Brunelleschi earned the unqualified praise of his contemporaries. His soaring dome, finished during his lifetime except for the lantern, and his geometric vision of space have fascinated generations of painters, sculptors and architects ever since.

Brunelleschi's dome was not just a technical and formal achievement: it punctuated the

Florentine skyline like an emblem of the Renaissance itself. Standing at the center of a shell-shaped valley crossed by the Arno, in between the hills of Fiesole and the foothills of the Galluzzo, it was in perfect harmony with the site. Instead of sealing the religious edifice like a lid, it surges skyward, dominating the city and, as Alberti put it, "covering with its shadow all the people of Tuscany." This formidable construction was, however, only one of Brunelleschi's accomplishments in Florence. While still working on the problem of the Cathedral dome, he built the Foundlings Hospital in 1419 according to the new laws of perspective and the requirements of town planning. The building is characterized by a great clarity in which the relations between all the parts can be expressed in terms of measurement. It occupies one side of the Piazza del Annunziata, onto which it opens with an arcade running along the entire facade. At San Lorenzo two years later, Brunelleschi created a synthesis of two classical architectural forms by designing the Old Sacristy as a cube crowned by a hemispherical cupola. For the church itself, he drew a simplified floor-plan that reproduces the forms of early Christian basilicas, a look backwards in another direction.

Brunelleschi's strength as an architect came from the mathematical rules which he applied to his buildings and the art of bringing out the relationships of the parts through the principles of perspective. He is famous for optical experiments in which he painted detailed views of the Baptistery and the Palazzo Vecchio: they were intended to be looked at in a mirror which could be seen only through a hole drilled in the center of the panel. With the reflected sky and clouds, the result was a perfect illusion. "These two works," Vasari reports, "awakened the intelligence of the other artists who afterwards began to study perspective with great application." Brunelleschi had paved the way towards a new representation of the world. The style he created was to dominate Florentine architecture for the next century. The ruler and the protractor reigned supreme, imposing symmetry and regularity throughout in the name of geometric beauty.

Michelozzo and the spreading of a style

While Brunelleschian canons became a source of inspiration to other architects from then on, there were many who sought to adapt them to the utilitarian demands of Florentine society and who themselves belonged to original or personal stylistic currents. One of these was Michelozzo di Bartolomeo (1396-1472), who trained as a

Above and opposite

FILIPPO BRUNELLESCHI
San Lorenzo
(interior: nave and capitals)
1421
Florence.

*The church of San Lorenzo has the
characteristic features of Brunelleschi's
architecture using a modular plan:
the square formed by the crossing of
the transepts is the basic unit. It
determines the dimensions of the
choir and of the transept arms. The
nave is composed of four such units.
Above the capitals, there is a carved
block which responds to the
entablature of the collateral aisles.*

goldsmith, worked as an engraver at the Florence Mint and then as a sculptor, before being led to architecture by his activities. Born the son of a tailor of Burgundian extraction, he was never given a theoretical education like Brunelleschi, nor was he endowed with the gifts of Donatello or Ghiberti, with whom he collaborated. His work, both plastic and architectural, was characterized by a certain persistent Gothicism, as we can see by the small convent church of San Francesco al Bosco in the Mugello district. His major constructions in Florence however, reflect an altogether different spirit.

At the request of Cosimo de' Medici, he rebuilt the monastery of San Marco and gave it what Vasari considered the most beautiful of cloisters. The regularity of the proportions, the simplicity of the decoration and the perfect ordering of the parts are all in keeping with the Renaissance vision. Michelozzo even distinguished himself by using Ionic capitals in the cloister and library, an order which had found little favor with Brunelleschi. His masterpiece in the realm of sacred architecture was the reconstruction of the Santa Annunziata church, which began in 1444 and ended in a great deal of controversy. Michelozzo opted for clarity and simplicity in his handling of space, restricting the decoration to capitals freely composed by a master-carver. Apart from these major projects, he was also entrusted with smaller works such as tabernacles and monuments, in which he experimented with new forms inspired from the Antique. His experience and his talent for functional architecture, as well as his taste in decoration, made him an obvious choice for Medici patronage. Between 1434 and 1439, he redesigned the Medici villas at Cafaggiolo and Careggi, and devised a new type of house for his patrons at Fiesole. He kept the fortress-like aspect of the villas with their covered walkways and machicolations—which he recycled into cornices—and made new, balanced openings in the walls. At Careggi, he graced the facade with a loggia above the portico.

Of all his private constructions, the Medici palace in the Via Larga (1444-1459) was the most influential. With its scantily-lit facades, variously accentuated stonework, and huge antique-style cornices giving it an imposing appearance, it became a model for all Florentine palaces. His greatest innovation was in the courtyard, which he ringed with a portico of classical columns, transposing the syntax of the cloister into an urban dwelling. Michelozzo created the basic design of the Renaissance Tuscan palace, reproducing it at the Palazzo Strozzino and in the *cortile* of the Palazzo Vecchio. Although influenced by Brunelleschi, he did

not hesitate to adapt the classical vocabulary to his personal taste, whether in Florence or other regions such as Lombardy, where his talent as sculptor came to the fore. Michelozzo thus actively contributed to spreading the new style, but Alberti was the one who opened yet newer horizons to architecture.

Alberti, theory and the universal man

With Brunelleschi, architecture became and art in its own right. Alberti, master-builder and theoretician, achieved a brilliant synthesis between Antiquity and the modern era, bringing architecture in relation with humanism. His wide-ranging education marked him as a prototypical Renaissance man. Born in Genoa in 1404 into a Florentine family in exile, he received a humanist education in Venice and Padua, then studied Law in Bologna. He was already thirty when he finally went to Florence, but he never stayed long, for he was a member of the pontifical court. Before turning to architecture he distinguished himself as a writer and theoretician, composing comedies, poems, amorous dialogues and treatises in defense of literature. His reflections on painting and sculpture, published in 1434, constituted a decisive prelude to his architectural speculations and to his practice of this new art form during the last thirty years of his life. Thanks to him, art and architecture, considered until then as merely a matter of technique, were granted a humanistic value on the same footing as ethics, history and poetry.

At the age of forty, he began writing a huge treatise, *De re aedificatoria*, in which he undertook a critical interpretation of Vitruvius. He drew two guiding principles from the work of his predecessor: the rightness of proportion in a building, and the analogy between buildings and the human body. In his words: "Proportion should govern the parts, so that they may give the appearance of a body perfect and whole, rather than a sum of incomplete and disjointed parts." After having established the pre-eminent role of architecture in the civic scheme of things, Alberti turned his attention to drawing and to the relations which it determined between mathematics and the art of building. He also gave thought to the question of materials and analyzed structural principles. Lastly, he considers the relationship between architecture and urbanism, and this he does consistently in reference to the art of Antiquity, whether in connection with public or private buildings, palaces or more modest dwellings. Alberti's ideas crystallized into a vision of an ideal city along Platonic lines, divided into twelve sections and ruled by the law of numbers. Given the paramount importance

Opposite and above (detail)

LEON BATTISTA ALBERTI
Santa Maria Novella
(view of the altered facade)
1458-1470)
Florence.

Designed by the greatest theoretician of architecture of the Renaissance, the facade of the church of Santa Maria Novella is a synthesis of classically-inspired composition and traditional Tuscan ornamental motifs. Alberti's invention of the volute, derived from the buttresses, serves as a harmonious junction between the various levels of the facade.

MICHELOZZO et DONATELLO
Exterior pulpit of the Cathedral
1428-1438, marble and bronze
Prato.

Opposite

LEON BATTISTA ALBERTI
Tempietto of the Holy Sepulcher
ca. 1455-1458
San Pancrazio, Florence.

This edifice commissioned by Giovanni Ruccella was modelled on the Holy Sepulcher in Jerusalem. Alberti borrowed elements from the Florence Baptistery and crowned his miniature replica with a cupola like its model in the Holy Land.

of the new funds of knowledge, he cast the architect into the role of an intellectual whose task was to achieve a clear, balanced and rational design in harmony with the demands of beauty.

The distance between idea and execution, separating the architect from the craftsman, explains why Leon Battista Alberti more often than not participated in a directive capacity and entrusted the actual construction to others: Bernardo Rossellino built the Palazzo Rucellai in Florence according to his instructions around 1446-1451, and Matteo dei Pasti used his plans to raise the Malatesta church in Rimini around 1447. Modernizing the facade of Santa Maria Novella in Florence, he left for posterity a model solution for the problem of balancing the vertical and horizontal elements, creating a harmonious junction between the different levels by adding two volutes structurally derived from the buttress, yet completely original by their geometric design.

Alberti's prime role in the history of architecture in general and of the Renaissance in particular was sustained by the numerous projects to which he contributed throughout Italy. Rome, Venice, Ferrara, Rimini, Mantua and Urbino, all could boast edifices built according to his plans. Alberti was not tempted to imitate himself, but gave free play to his inventiveness, all the while arriving at solutions that proved to be of enduring value: the superimposition of orders at the Palazzo Rucellai, three main types of church facades, and three new types of floor-plan—the Greek cross, and a combination of nave plus rotunda—were features shared by many of Alberti's buildings, and all were characterized by an exemplary boldness.

BERNARDO ROSSELLINO
The Town Square of Pienza
On the left, the Cathedral;
on the right, the Piccolomini
Palace,
1460–1462.

*Bernardo Rossellino, former
collaborator of Alberti at the Palazzo
Rucellai in Florence, also worked at
the Vatican and was commissioned
by Pius II to transform Corsignano
into a bishop's residence. In less than
three years, Pienza became the city
to be built along "ideal" Renaissance
lines. Each building in the town-
plan corresponded to a specific type of
architecture. The Cathedral was built
according to the "hall-church" plan
popular in Southern Germany. The
Piccolomini Palace, however, is
practically a direct quotation of
Alberti's Rucellai Palace.*

Opposite

MICHELOZZO
**The Palazzo Communale of
Montepulciano**
Facade from the 15th century.

Ghiberti

and

narrative bas-relief

With Leon Battista Alberti, Lorenzo Ghiberti was among the personalities of the Quattrocento who best exemplified the ideal of what we today call the "Renaissance man," one whose knowledge was equalled only by his thirst for more. In the memoirs, or *Commentarii*, he wrote in his later years, the first autobiography by an artist–he demonstrated his culture by basing his history of art on the classical texts of Pliny, Varro and Vitruvius, and expounded on his self-wrought theory of proportions. Ghiberti made no secret of his passionate involvement in the arts. He sought the company of artists and scholars alike, and was himself a great collector of antique objets d'art. Distinguishing himself in the disciplines of painting, drawing, sculpture, architecture and precious metalwork, he was acutely conscious of his own worth. In the highly-charged atmosphere of Florence, where figures like Donatello valued criticism more than admiration, Ghiberti took up the defense of his own art and set out to justify it in all the major projects of the day. The wealth of material he provided in his *Commentarii* shows that he was aware of living in exceptional times and of participating both spiritually and artistically in a veritable rebirth.

LORENZO GHIBERTI
East Door of the Baptistery
(detail of self-portrait)
ca. 1445-1448, gilt bronze, Florence.

The self-portrait, which Ghiberti included among the heads of prophets and other biblical figures framing the panels of the "Gates of Paradise", depicts his likeness with great naturalism. It is a far cry from the self-portrait which the sculptor made for the North Door of the Baptistery and which is closer to classical prototypes.

After a brief stay in Pesaro in 1400 to flee the plague and the political upheavals in Florence, and also to execute paintings for the Malatesta court, Ghiberti's debut as an artist was marked by a stunning success in 1401. In that year the city of Florence organized a great contest for the second Baptistery door calling for the participation of the best sculptors in Tuscany. Among them were the Sienese masters Jacopo della Quercia and Francesco di Valdambrino, the Florentine goldsmiths Brunelleschi, Ghiberti, Simone da Colle Valdelsa and Niccolo d'Arezzo, as well as the young Donato. The candidates in this high-level competition–which put an end to the Gothic age in which they had all been schooled–were given twelve months to match their talent to the door executed by Andrea Pisano seventy years before.

The subject chosen for the trial piece to be submitted was the *Sacrifice of Abraham*, described in great detail, even down to the number of figures to be represented. Jacopo della Quercia's work, the one most strongly marked still by the Gothic style, with its strong contrasts and sharp relief, was considered lacking in finesse. In the end, Ghiberti's only serious rival was Brunelleschi, future architect of the Cathedral's dome, who placed Isaac in the center of the panel and the other figures all around. The opposition of Abraham and the Angel on either side of him lent a great dramatic force to the scene. Brunelleschi however, was criticized for having created too frontal a composition and for having used up all the available space. Also, by casting the figures separately and then assembling on the background, as Andrea Pisano had done, no effect of depth was achieved. Ghiberti on the other hand, put the main scene to one side and separated the figures into two groups along a diagonal axis. More importantly, by casting the figures along with the background, he created a unified composition and heightened the effect of illusionistic space. Only the figure of Isaac was cast separately and more finely worked, thus enhancing its essential role in the scene. In choosing Lorenzo Ghiberti as the winner, the jury was not rewarding the most innovative of the sculptors; by the dramatic force of his composition and its symmetrical organization, Brunelleschi was definitely the more modern of the two. But the internal narrative coherence, the pictorial conception of the panel and the elegance of the figure tipped the scales in Ghiberti's favor. His life's work was off to a brilliant start.

For Ghiberti and for the other artists of his circle, the outcome of the 1401 contest marked the beginning of a new era. The work on the second, or north door of the

LORENZO GHIBERTI
The Sacrifice of Abraham
(panel for the Baptistery door contest)
1401, gilt bronze
53.3 x 44.5 cm
Museo Nazionale (Bargello), Florence.

Of all the panels submitted for the Baptistery door contest of 1401, only those of Ghiberti and Brunelleschi have been preserved. Ghiberti's panel displays great pictorial and visual unity. The Gothic-proportioned figures–only that of Isaac embodies the Classical ideal–create a lively scene in which light and landscape play an important part.

Above and opposite (detail)

LORENZO GHIBERTI
**The Story of Adam and Eve
Panel from the East Door
of the Baptistery**
1425-1437, gilt bronze,
79.5 x 79.5 cm.
Museo dell'Opera del Duomo,
Florence.

*This panel combines four scenes from
Genesis: the Creation of Adam, the
Creation of Eve, the Temptation,
and the Expulsion. The influence of
Antiquity is visible in the figure of
Eve set in the pose of* Venus
Pudica.

Baptistery, which lasted over twenty years, from 1402 to 1424, brought Ghiberti into contact with the greatest bronzesmiths, decorators and master painters like Paolo Uccello. The door to which he devoted almost a quarter of a century was divided into twenty-eight quadrilobed panels, like Andrea Pisano's. Twenty of them depicted scenes from the life of Christ, while the remaining eight portrayed the four evangelists and the Fathers of the Church. Where Pisano had decorated the frames with rosette, point and lion's head ornaments, Ghiberti designed a continuous band of intertwined ivy with heads of different prophets and sibyls at the corner of each panel. The door jambs and architraves were graced with garlands of flowers and fruit. In each of the panels, the sculptural talent which he had displayed in the *Sacrifice of Abraham* was brought to fruition. Set against architectural or landscape backgrounds, the figures are clearly positioned in depth, and many are in high-relief. The whole demonstrates not just a great technical ability, but also a remarkable imagination and a supreme elegance in the handling of the subject-matter. The existing sketches for the *Flagellation of Christ* show how he and his assistants proceeded in rendering plastic effects. The movements of the bodies and contrasts of light and shadow before casting figures as exquisite as those of the Parisian ivory-carvers. To be sure, the project which occupied Ghiberti for so many years served to train and nurture an entire generation of artists. By the year 1407, he had a team of over twenty-five assistants, including the likes of Uccello, Michelozzo, Donatello, and Bernardo Ciuffagni, who has unjustly lapsed into oblivion.

While Ghiberti was working on the Baptistery door, a new wave of sculptors was coming to the fore in Florence. Donatello and Nanni di Ranco graced the Duomo with their masterpieces and at the bequest of the guilds, executed statues for the niches of Or' San Michele. Following an injunction by his own guild, the Calimala, Ghiberti contributed to this project an impressive bronze *Saint John the Baptist* which was cast in a single piece. Although a veritable technical feat, the unwieldiness of the figure led Ghiberti to restrict himself in the future to works of a smaller format and with more fluid contours.

Through his exposure to the works of Brunelleschi and Donatello, Ghiberti was able to find his way to a new manner of representing space in relief. In his bronze reliefs for the Baptistery of Siena, executed between 1417 and 1427, he showed his openness to the new stylistic tendencies by applying the principles of linear perspective to his compositions. In scenes like *St. John the Baptist before Herod* and the *Baptism of Christ*, increased the narrative impact, all

Above and opposite (detail)

LORENZO GHIBERTI
**The Story of Adam and Eve
Panel from the East Door
of the Baptistery**
1425–1437, gilt bronze,
79.5 x 79.5 cm.
Museo dell'Opera del Duomo,
Florence.

*Instead of the traditional 28-panel
format adopted on the other
Baptistery doors, Leonardo Bruni's
program for the East Door, called the
"Gate of Paradise," reduced the
number of panels to ten, further
increasing the narrative challenge for
the sculptor.*

Above and opposite (detail)

LORENZO GHIBERTI
**The Story of David and
Goliath
Panel from the East Door
of the Baptistery**
1425-1437, gilt bronze,
79.5 x 79.5 cm.
Museo dell'Opera del Duomo,
Florence.

*The panels of the East Door are the
most perfect expression of the
Renaissance style in the field of the
bas-relief.*

LORENZO GHIBERTI
The Gates of Paradise
1425-1452, bronze,
457 x 251 (without frame),
East Door of the Baptistery,
Florence.

Opposite

LORENZO GHIBERTI
**The Story of David and
Goliath** (detail)

the while enhancing the harmony of line and gradation of planes. This new approach was a radical departure from the style he adopted for the north door in Florence. He explored during this period all the possibilities of narrative bas-relief, and these experiments permitted him to try yet a new direction which he brought to perfection in the third, or east door of the same Baptistery. This door, which became known as the Gate of Paradise, was executed after a program established by Leonardo Bruni that called for a modification of the general lay-out. In reducing the number of panels from twenty-eight to ten, Ghiberti was faced with the task of representing several different events in a single composition and a devising a new system of execution to link the sequences into a whole. The result was a triumph in narrative bas-relief, with scenes artfully combined for maximum dramatic effect. Organized according to the laws of perspective, the architectural or landscape settings brought great clarity to various scenes represented. The ten reliefs were finished in 1440, but the marginal figures, frames and technical solutions were not ready before the spring of 1452 at the same time as the gilding. The beauty of this work generated so much enthusiasm and admiration that it was decided to install the panels on the side facing the Cathedral and to move Andrea Pisano's door to the south side. Michelangelo himself found it worthy of being the Gate to Paradise. In his memoirs, Ghiberti wrote: "Of all the works I created, this was the most extraordinary; it was executed with the greatest skill, the greatest balance, and the utmost inventiveness." By mid-century, Ghiberti had managed to combine the crafts of goldsmith and sculptor in a single work, and paved the way to a truly new vision of sculpture.

Sculpture
and Inspiration
from the Antique

At the beginning of the 15th century, at a time when the Church was practically the only patron, sculpture played primarily a religious or decorative role in iconographic programs. Destined for altars, tombs and gates, its range of subject matter was limited: the main figures on which artists could exercise their talents were those of Christ, the Virgin the saints and allegories of the Virtues; nudes were restricted to Adam and Eve and St. Sebastian, and portraits to tomb sculpture. Sculptors had an even smaller margin of freedom than painters, but could circumvent their clients' vigilance when they worked for confraternities and other organizations. The re-emergence of profane sculpture was a slow process: signs of a renewal became evident only toward mid-century, as the return to the art of Antiquity brought with it a rebirth of portraiture. Discreetly, profane sculpture made its reappearance at first in private houses. Donatello's *David* already stood in the courtyard of Cosimo de' Medici's palace. But it was not until the end of the century that such sculptures were to be offered to the public eye in the squares and gardens of Florence.

The religious vocation of sculpture then made it difficult for artists to turn wholeheartedly to Antique statuary, which was dominated by the nude and the portrait. What they drew upon was more its appearance than

Above and opposite (detail)

DONATELLO
David
(detail of head)
ca. 1440-1443, bronze,
Height: 158.2 cm.
Museo Nazionale (Bargello),
Florence.

Donatello's most famous bronze, probably executed shortly before his departure to Padua, was originally placed in the courtyard of the Medici palace. The classicism of this mature work is tempered by an exceptional softness of form.

95

its principles. One major borrowing was the classic *contrapposto* pose, in which the figure's weight rests on one leg and one shoulder is higher than the other. Adopted also was the principle of modular proportions. Finally, the great themes of classical sculpture came back into favor: the male nude by far more widespread the female nude, the equestrian statue and the portrait bust. Another rediscovery was the prestige of bronze–in fashion throughout Antiquity but virtually ignored by the Middle Ages–and a taste for naturalism which decisively distinguishes Renaissance art from that of the Gothic.

Jacopo della Quercia and Nanni di Banco: Creators of a new style

While Florence was in the vanguard during the first half of the 15th century in the field of sculpture, it was a Sienese sculptor, Jacopo della Quercia (1374-1438), who took the first steps in the new direction. His entry for the Baptistery door contest of 1401 has not come down to us, but his marble *Tomb of Ilaria del Carretto*, executed in 1406 with Francesco da Valdambrino for the Cathedral of Lucca, displays all the boldness of his vision. Based on an antique sarcophagus preserved at the Camposanto in Pisa, it is topped by a recumbent portrait of the deceased: the face of the dead woman is full of serenity, and the folds of her dress are treated in such a way as to create a harmonious ensemble. The heavy garland–held by winged cherubs that rings the sarcophagus on all four sides–lends a graceful, ornamental touch to the whole.

Commissioned by Siena, between 1409 and 1419, Jacopo della Quercia executed the *Fonte Gaia*, a monumental fountain with free-standing statues of Rea Silvia and Acca Larentia that symbolized the city's connection with Roman Antiquity. The sculptor added a figure of the Madonna surrounded by allegorical representations of the Virtues and scenes from the life of Adam. He displayed great originality in combining the classical style with female figures in Gothic-style attitudes. Yet by its simplicity, monumental formality and emphatic expressivity, Jacopo della Quercia's work marked a decisive break with the gothic world and achieved a remarkable fullness which was later to fascinate Michelangelo.

While Jacopo della Quercia pursued his career in various cities in Tuscany, most of the major sculptors of the Quattrocento converged on Florence. Where work on the Duomo required master craftsmen of all kinds and artists of different generations. The vast scale of the project led to a great diversity in production and constant opportunities for collaboration between artists of different origins.

One example of these was Nanni di Banco (ca. 1380-1421) who worked at the Duomo for over fifteen years side by side with Donatello. Entrusted with similar commissions, they were faced with similar problems. Nanni apprenticed in the workshop of his father Antonio di Banco, a stone-carver who later worked on the Cathedral as an architect. Father and son worked together on the decoration of the door of the Mandorla in 1407, but Nanni executed alone in the following year the figure of a prophet for the tribune. His synthesis of Gothic art and classical Antiquity on this occasion provided the first taste of what was to be a very personal style in which he fully asserted his temperament. His originality further manifested itself in that same year when he was called upon to execute one of the four monumental figures of the evangelists to be placed in niches on the facade of Santa Maria del Fiore. *Saint Mark* was entrusted to Niccolo di Pietro Lamberti, *Saint Matthew* to Bernardo Ciuffagni, *Saint John* to Donatello, and *Saint Luke* to Nanni di Banco. The first two, Lamberti and Ciuffagni, produced works still harking back to the Gothic tradition, but Nanni di Banco demonstrated his originality by carving his figure in relation to its placement. By giving his *Saint Luke* a slight twist avoiding strict frontality, he created a more natural pose reinforced by the expressive facial features and by a treatment of drapery that follows the anatomical contours. The figure's gaze is cast downward to respond to that of the spectator. Nanni succeeded with a work both monumental and lively and as emotionally effective as Donatello's, yet more gentle.

Nanni di Banco's talent was duly appreciated, and he was entrusted–along with Ghiberti and Donatello–with the execution of the statues of the guilds for the niches on the outer walls of Or' San Michele. Between 1411 and 1414, he sculpted *Saint Philip* for the shoemakers' guild, *Saint Aloysius* for the blacksmith's guild, and the group of *Four Crowned Saints* for the stone-carvers' guild, to which he of course belonged himself. He met the challenge of bringing four figures together in a single niche by grouping them into a solemn colloquy, giving the saints the appearance of Antique statues. In a further homage to Antiquity, Nanni executed figures in high-relief for the base of the niche. Until his death in 1421, Nanni di Banco continued to work in the direction which he had initiated. Although lacking the vivacity of Donatello, he could confer a tremendous feeling of movement to his figures, and perhaps nowhere more so than in his *Assumption of the Virgin* for the tympanum of the door of the Mandorla. In depicting his main figure held up by angels, free of all materiality, Nanni di Banco achieved a true synthesis of the values of sacred Medieval art and the spirit of the Renaissance.

NICCOLO DI PIETRO LAMBERTI
Saint Mark
1410-1412, marble,
Museo dell'Opera del Duomo,
Florence

BERNARDO CIUFFAGNI
Saint Matthew
1410, marble,
Museo dell'Opera del Duomo,
Florence

DONATELLO
Saint John the Evangelist
ca. 1412-1415, marble,
Height: 210 cm
Museo dell'Opera del Duomo,
Florence

NANNI DI BANCO
Saint Luke
1408-1412, marble,
Height: 208 cm
Museo dell'Opera del Duomo,
Florence

His disappearance highlighted all the more the personality of another artist who, by himself, became the most representative of the Italian Renaissance sculptors of the second quarter of the 15th century.

Donatello and naturalism

Donatello (ca. 1383-1466) is associated with the golden age of Florence, where he participated in most of its great works and was closely acquainted with Brunelleschi, Ghiberti and Michelozzo, but his fame and influence spread largely beyond his native Tuscany. Little is known about his apprenticeship or how he embarked on such a long career marked by so many prestigious accomplishments. Among these were three saints for the niches of Or' San Michele (1411-1423), four prophets and the *Isaac and Abraham* group for the Cathedral bell-tower (1415-1436), the tomb sculptures for cardinal Cossa at the Baptistery and for cardinal Brancacci in Naples (1421-1431), a relief and bronze figures for the baptismal fonts of Siena (1423-1429), the outdoor pulpit for the Cathedral of Prato, and the *Cantoria* of the Duomo in Florence on which he worked for ten years beginning in 1428; also to his credit are the bronze doors and pendentive medallions of the Sacristy of San Lorenzo, and bronze thrones in this same church. In Padua, between 1443 and 1453, he executed the equestrian monument of *Gattamelata* and a monumental ensemble for the altar of the basilica of San Antonio. In addition to these religious works, Donatello enjoyed private commissions from his early patrons and sponsor, the Martelli, and from Cosimo de' Medici, who in Vasari's words, "held him in such high esteem that he never stopped giving him work."

At the major sites that occupied Florentine artists–the Cathedral and Or' San Michele–Donatello immediately set him self off from his contemporaries. His first statues, all in marble and of a religious character, displayed the distinguishing traits of his art; namely intensity of expression and dynamic form. Where classical sculpture had sought to express serenity, harmony and the ideal, Donatello strove above all to express feelings. He took from antique statuary the principles of composition and proportion, fluid movement, and the polished surfaces of marble and bronze. But he adopted a resolutely personal stance when it came to treating the subject and conceiving the work in its context. By working in Venice, Ferrara, Prato, Siena and Rome, the sculptor assimilated different techniques and tried out a variety of manners in his figures. His influence was considerable, even though none of his pupils

managed to surpass him. Unlike Alberti, Brunelleschi, and even Ghiberti–typically well-rounded Renaissance men–Donatello limited his efforts to sculpture. His involvement in architecture did not go beyond the execution of thrones, tribunes and decorative elements. His preferred materials for statues were marble and bronze, and for bas-reliefs generally the latter. Only four of his statues were carved out of wood, the traditional material for Italian religious sculpture. As for genres, he soon abandoned funerary monuments, executed few reliquary busts and figures, and totally neglected fashionable small-format statuary. At first glance, the artist's range might seem quite narrow.

On the other hand, his works freed themselves little by little from the simple function of representation and from pre-established contexts. By the way it was positioned in space and granted specific expressivity, the statue gained an impressive presence which directly implicated the spectator. Large-format statuary gave Donatello the opportunity to master the depiction of poses, costume and facial expression. Bas-relief was his proving ground for the treatment of space and perspective. In both fields of endeavor he gradually abandoned marble in favor of bronze, which lent itself better to technical innovation. Progressively too, his statues edged beyond their confining frames to stand on their own. The *Prophets* of the campanile (1433), part of his first generation of works, are still ensconced in their niches, but the *Gattamelata* in Padua (1444) and his *Judith and Holophernes*. both on cylindrical pedestals, were intended to be seen on all sides. A faithful follower of the Antique in his practice of the bas-relief, he perfected the technique by introducing linear perspective and heightened the illusionistic effect by varying the degree of relief from the foreground to the background (*rilievo schiacciato*) to unify the scenes and create a more intense dramatic coherence.

If there is one feature which characterizes Donatello's sculpture from beginning to end, it is its expressive naturalism. Sustained by his perfect technical mastery, he was able to transpose into marble, bronze or wood a wide range of feeling in all their complexity. By its pose and facial type, the *Saint George* he carved in marble for Or' San Michele, gives the impression of calm energy. The *Habakuk* of the campanile already seems prey to visions. His bronze *David* nonchalantly displays a smooth, youthful body whose nakedness requires only light for its adornment. Serene bodies, gentleness of mien, and poetic grace were not Donatello's main concern. If anything, his figures stand for passion, violence, suffering and a savage beauty meant to inspire awe.

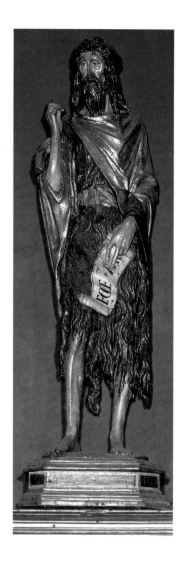

DONATELLO
Saint John the Baptist
1438, gilt and painted wood,
141 cm.
Santa Maria Gloriosa dei Frati,
Venice.

Opposite

DONATELLO
Saint John the Baptist
Marble.
Museo Nazionale (Bargello),
Florence.

His *Maria Magdalena* executed for the Baptistery in 1455, is the image of the sculptor's own spiritual tenor. To render the Magdalena's physical decrepitude and spiritual crisis he chose the traditional material of religious sculpture—wood. But in this last finished work, he handled the wood as if it were bronze to stress the interplay of movement, form and light. With an extraordinary power, he reasserted his artistic convictions by exercising his sense of detail to a paradoxical degree and conferring to the penitent saint's emaciated face a mystical meaning. It was such demonstrations of vigor that so impressed his contemporaries, even though his art often seems to deviate from the Renaissance spirit and works of a new style and great gentleness which were pouring out of the studio of Luca della Robbia.

Above and opposite (detail)

DONATELLO
Mary Magdalene
(formerly in the Baptistery)
ca. 1453-1455, gilt and
painted wood,
185 cm.
Museo dell'Opera del Duomo,
Florence.

Above and opposite (detail)

DONATELLO (?)
Niccolo da Uzzano
ca. 1430, painted terracotta,
46 cm.
Museo Nazionale(Bargello),
Florence.

*Among the problematic works
attributed to Donatello is this
antique-style bust of the humanist
banker Niccolo da Uzzano.
The head was executed after
a life- or death-mask.*

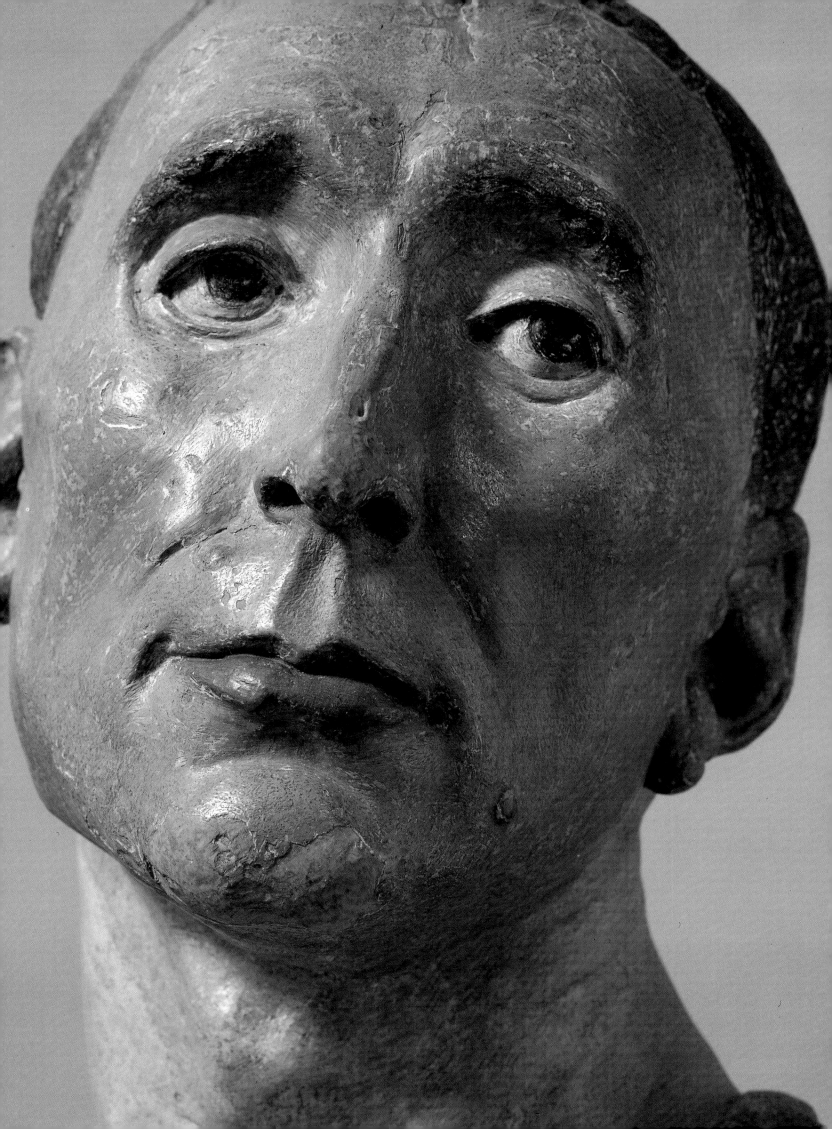

Luca della Robbia
and
the Decorative Arts

*W*hen Leon Battista Alberti, upon his return to Florence, praised the grandeur and beauty of the artistic movement which was opening a new world, the names which he associated with this marvellous rebirth were those of the architect Brunelleschi the painter Masaccio, the sculptors Ghiberti and Donatello, and another who had only just begun to show what he was capable of: Luca della Robbia. In comparison with the tumultuous power of Donatello however, this young sculptor worked in a more serene register and seems to have found his models in the fluidity and harmony of the sculpture of Nanni di Banco.

        Luca della Robbia, born at the beginning of the 15th century in a distinguished Florentine family, was trained as a goldsmith but none of his early works have come down to us. He may have collaborated with Nanni di Banco on the typanum representing the *Assumption of the Virgin* at the door of the Mandorla. In any event, the fact that in 1431 he was entrusted with the execution of a *Cantoria* in the Cathedral of Santa Maria del Fiore, shows that his talent was certainly recognized by then. Finished in 1438, this singing loft was a fitting pendant to the one executed by Donatello. The subject which Luca carved into marble was Psalm 150, *Laudate Dominicum*, the text of which was inscribed in Roman script on the entablatures and base. The

reliefs are all literal illustrations of the biblical verses. The groups of children are divided into panels emphatically separated by double-pilasters and according to their part in the choir. They sing the psalm with the accompaniment of trumpets, tambourines, bells, an organ, a harp and other string instruments. In comparison with the Dionysian movement which animates the figures of Donatello, these groups of children are full of charm, and their faces, with their rounded features and open expressions, recall the angels of Nanni di Banco, expressing a perfect joy and harmony. Luca della Robbia's drapery here has all of the nobility of the costumes on Ghiberti's figures, but with much more naturalness. For these singing and dancing cherubs, music seems to be a form of purification.

Working between 1440 and 1446 on the bronze doors of the New Sacristy in the Duomo in collaboration with Michelozzo and Maso di Bartolomeo, Luca della Robbia set himself off even more from the straightforward style of Donatello through his balanced compositions and serenely solemn groups. He achieved this by organizing each of the ten panels around a main figure flanked by two angels. In this work there is a perfect mastery in the fluid modeling of the figures, the harmony of the gestures, the curving contours of the arms, and the finely-carved folds of the drapery.

With so much skill at his disposal, it is no wonder that he was able to perfect the technique of painted and glazed terracotta to popularize his bas-relief designs. Starting in 1440, after having worked successfully in marble and bronze, the sculptor devoted his efforts primarily to this new technique. It was then that he established the famous ceramic workshop that also employed his nephew Andrea (1435-1525), and later Andrea's sons Giovanni (1469-1529) and Girolamo (1488-1566), who perpetuated its fame into the Cinquecento.

Vasari attributes to Luca della Robbia the rediscovery, application and experimental development of this technique. In fact, it had already been known in Mesopotamia, and often used by the Persians and Arabs, but Luca extended its application to statuary. Terracotta covered with glazed enamel has the advantage of great resistance to weathering and virtually unalterable colors. Appealing by its novelty, it had the further advantage of low cost and reproducibility. This technique could be applied to objects of small size as well as to compositions rivaling with major statuary and painting, and of course to large-scale architectural decoration. Works in glazed terracotta may accordingly be

LUCA DELLA ROBBIA
Cantoria (detail)

*The children's faces, full of charm
and candour, are transfigured
by the music, as in a rite
of purification. They express
the blessing of perfect harmony.*

found on pediments for doors or tabernacles, in niches, medallions, *tondi*, coats-of-arms, or simply as busts.

Apart from the practical considerations that led Luca della Robbia to elaborate on this invention, the most compelling reasons were of an artistic order, for it permitted the sculptor to explore the extra dimension of color in all its brilliance. In most of his compositions, Luca placed figures of an immaculate whiteness against a blue background, saving the greens and yellows, or browns and pinks for accessory details. Whether of sacred subjects or profane, the glazed terracotta works that came out of his *bottega*, or workshop, all featured one or more white enamel figures against a field of blue, in contrast to the lush garlands of leaves and fruit which served as frames and were treated naturalistically. The appeal of Luca della Robbia's ceramic works comes not just from the cool white surfaces, the lavender-blue and the raw green enamels, but also from the extreme delicacy of the modeling, the simplicity of the lifelike forms, and the directness of the painted eyes. Luca systematically exploited all of the possibilities of painted and glazed terracotta and executed remarkable decorative ensembles for some of the most prestigious constructions of the Florentine Renaissance: the Pazzi Chapel at Santa Croce, which he decorated with medallions of the evangelists, and the vaults of the chapel of the cardinal of Portugal at San Miniato al Monte, which display *tondi* representing the *Trinity* and the *Cardinal Virtues*.

This art form earned the recognition of the great master and became very popular when Andrea della Robbia, his nephew and closest collaborator, succeeded Luca as head of the workshop. The new productions which came out of the *bottega* had none of the simplicity of its founder's style, but reproduced clichés from Florentine painting of the period. As more and more orders poured in, invention was sacrificed to mass-production. With the exception of the poignant figures of infants in swaddling clothes executed for the medallions of the Foundling's Hospital (1463-1466), Andrea della Robbia tended to repeat himself or the compositions of Ghirlandaio, Lorenzo di Credi, or other Tuscan painters. The effects may have been more spectacular or elaborate, but much was left to be desired in the way of good taste.

Considering the works that came out of Luca della Robbia's workshop, it is evident that the Florentine Renaissance not only affected the production of so-called High Art, but also influenced the decorative arts quite directly. In some cases, the Quattrocento only grafted its new style onto fields which the Medieval craftsmen had already perfectly mastered; in other cases, like that of Luca della Robbia, it led to the rediscovery of ancient techniques and

Opposite

ANDREA DELLA ROBBIA
Bust of a Boy
ca. 1470, enamelled terracotta,
Height: 33 cm.
Museo Nazionale (Bargello),
Florence.

Above and opposite

LUCA DELLA ROBBIA
Madonna of the Roses
1450–1460, enamelled terracotta,
Museo Nazionale (Bargello)
Florence.

ANDREA DELLA ROBBIA
Madonna of the Stone-carvers
1475-1480, enamelled terracotta,
134 x 96 cm.
Museo Nazionale (Bargello),
Florence.

*In the ceramic workshop run
by the artist's family, the High Art
of the Renaissance was turned out
on an industrial scale. The theme
of the Virgin and Child was offered
in a number of variations. The taste
for naturalism reached its culmination
in the* Madonna of the Stone-
carvers, *whose frame is composed
of a generous garland of flowers.*

helped develop new forms of expression. Despite the adoption of new iconography, some decorative arts like stained-glass and illumination lost ground in favor of painting. Precious metalwork lost the prominence it had during the Middle Ages, even though the workshops continued to be very active and to offer a choice training-ground for artists who later made their mark in painting. Thanks to the many publications on geometric ornamentation and experimentation with perspective, marquetry became very much in demand as did majolica, for which Florence became a leading center thanks to the works of Luca della Robbia, which appealed to a large public and later to no less of a poet than Rilke: "There especially in the works of Andrea, Luca and sometimes Giovanni, where the colors are reduced to just a few, where an exquisite blue seems to transfigure the dazzling white of the angel heads, or elsewhere, to content itself with introducing on the side mainly in the festoons–a discreet quickening, like the pious hymn of a time more colored in this very pure harmony, there one can be touched by a magic which spans the centuries."

·R·P·
BENOTII DE FEDE
RIGIS EPI FESVLANI
QVI VIR INTEGERIMAE
VITAE SVMA CVM LAVDE
VIXIT ANNO QVE
M·CCCCL· DEFVN
CTVS EST

Painting: Art and Science

Along with Masaccio and Piero della Francesca, Paolo Uccello appears as one of the most striking personalities of the Florentine Renaissance, one who strove constantly to achieve purity of form and expression. Although much respected by the other artists of his time, he was often criticized by them for his systematic quest for rules. During a period dominated by the rational order of Brunelleschi and by the achievements of Masaccio and Donatello, Paolo Uccello was haunted by speculations on linear perspective and an acute sensitivity to the plasticity of forms. His work is striking because fantastic.

Paolo Uccello: apprentice goldsmith

Seven years after his birth in Florence in 1397, the son of a barber and surgeon, Paolo Uccello worked as a *garzone di bottega* in Ghiberti's studio in the company of men like Masolino, Donatello and Michelozzo. When his master executed his first door for the Baptistery, Paolo was among those who modestly contributed to its completion for the equally modest salary of five florins a year. At the age of eighteen he was enrolled in the Arte de Medici e speciali and lived in the parish of Santa Maria Nepoticosa. In 1424, along with Masaccio, he was admitted into the San Luca painters' guild.

Opposite

PAOLO UCCELLO
The Resurrection
1443-1444, stained-glass window
on the Cathedral dome.
Diameter: 468 cm.
Santa Maria del Fiore, Florence.

125

Uccello was trained not only as a goldsmith and a painter, but also as a mosaicist, and it was in this capacity that he was summoned to Venice to re-lay the mosaics that had been destroyed by fire in the basilica of San Marco. Taking over from Jacobello della Chiesa he worked there for five years until 1430, before returning to Florence, then captivated by Masaccio. Where his stint in Northern Italy had exposed him to the last stirrings of Late Gothic art, Tuscany at the time of his return was entirely dominated by the new pictorial revolution, whose principles had been established by Brunelleschi and put into practice by Masaccio and Donatello. In 1432, he applied for work at Santa Maria del Fiore and the supervisory council wrote to the Florentine ambassador in Venice to enquire on the quality and prices of "a certain Paolo Dono from Florence, master mosaicist, who executed a figure of Saint Peter for a facade of San Marco's in Venice." For the next few years he was employed at the Cathedral and in projects at various Florentine churches. In 1436 he signed his first major work, the *Equestrian Monument* to the famous English *condottiere* John Hawkwood, whom the Italians re-christened Giovanni Acuty. It was in that same year that Alberti put the finishing touches to his *Treatise on Painting* which he dedicated to Filippo Brunelleschi.

In 1394, the Signoria of Florence had wanted to manifest the city's gratitude to the condottiere who had led its troops to victory at Casaria by erecting a monument in the Duomo. The initial project calling for a marble statue was rather quickly abandoned in favor of a fresco that was entrusted to Agnolo Gaddi and Giuliano d'Arrigo. The result of this first effort must not have been to the liking of the City Fathers, for Uccello was called in to cover the figures of man and horse and to start again from scratch—a pentimento which occasioned the renewal of commemorative wall-painting.

Uccello dispatched his task in a matter of weeks, with spectacular results. Spread over 40 square meters of wall space, the monumental equestrian portrait of the condottiere gives the illusion of statuary in the round. He achieved this in two ways. First, he depicted figurative objects that reinforce the idea of the monument: the horse indicates the hero's social rank, while the tomb underscores the nature of the city's homage. The form of the sarcophagus and its inscription were honors that were formerly conferred only upon distinguished military leaders of Antiquity or emperors. Secondly, the equestrian group, which stands in solemn equilibrium, was elaborated according to the laws of perspective. Actually, the architectural base and the figures above are depicted according to different points of view: the

PAOLO UCCELLO
**The Battle of San Romano:
Bernardino della Ciarda
Unhorsed**
1456, oil on wood,
182 x 323 cm.
Galleria degli Uffizi, Florence.

*The three panels depicting the victory
of the Florentines over the Sienese at
San Romano were originally hung in
the chamber of Lorenzo de' Medici.*

Opposite

PAOLO UCCELLO
**The Battle of San Romano:
Bernardino della Ciarda
Unhorsed** (detail)

man and horse are represented as if at eye-level, while the pedestal is shown as if seen from below. The quality of the *Monument to Sir John Hawkwood* so appealed to his patrons at the Cathedral, that Uccello was commissioned for further work in 1443, as described by his biographer Vasari: "In the same period an in the same church, he painted in fresco on the inside of the facade, above the main portal, a clock with four heads in the corners." He was also asked to sketch designs for the round windows of the dome, as Ghiberti, Donatello and Andrea del Castagno had also been commissioned to do. His design for the *Resurrection* displays many characteristic features of his work: the distribution of figures in space, the perspective handling of the sarcophagus, the dramatic intensity, and lastly the presence of the *mazzocchio*, a Florentine headpiece made of wood or tressed reeds used as a support for draped bonnets or scarves. The mazzocchio was one of Uccello's favorite pictorial objects because of its geometric properties which lent themselves so well to the play of perspective, which was worked out here in the manner of Piero della Francesca, who dealt with this problem in his *Treatise on Perspective*. Despite loyal criticism from his friend Donatello, who reproached him for abandoning "the known for the unknown," Paolo devoted much time to drawing polyhedrons.

Perspective and problems in optics

Uccello's impassioned inquiry into perspective led him to deviate from the principles laid down by Brunelleschi and approach the optical problems in other ways. His fresco cycle for Santa Maria Novella depicting *Genesis* and *The Flood*, although no longer in their original state, give a good idea of the extent and tenor of his imagination. Instead of the one-point perspective scheme then in vogue among artists, he used the natural, or descriptive perspective so dear to Ghiberti and derived from medieval ideas on optics. He adopted different vanishing points for each subject or group of objects. Vasari wrote: "He represented the dead, the tempest, the fury of the winds, lightning bolts, splintered trees, and the terror of the living with such care and skill that scarce more need be said... He decreased the size of the figures according to the play of perspective lines and executed several *mazzocchi* and other delightful pieces of bravura." His depiction of *The Flood* presents an impressive and obsessive perspective construction which draws the spectator's gaze inexorably towards the abysmal depths. The drama is set between the towering sides of the Arch, where figures struggle with their last strength to stave off their doom.

The elements in upheaval play havoc with the normal optical effects: an unreal light seems to bathe the pathetic bodies painted in a grisaille that intensifies the shadows. Monumentality and perspective found their ultimate expression in Paolo Uccello's most famous work, the three panels of the Battle of San Romano commissioned by Cosimo de' Medici and executed in the middle of the Quattrocento. The subject of this masterpiece is the decisive battle in which Niccolo da Tolentino led the Florentines to victory against their Sienese foes commanded by Bernardino della Ciarda on the 1st of June, 1432. Uccello divided it into three episodes: Niccolo Mauruzi da Tolentino at the head of his troops; the counter-attack by Micheletto Attendolo da Cotignola that turned the tide; and the final defeat of the enemy by the un-horsing of Bernardino della Ciarda. The three panels, today dispersed in London, Paris and Florence, constituted a commemorative cycle which once decorated a room of the Medici palace built by Michelozzo. The episodes of the *Battle of San Romano* highlight the role of the condottieri in the great tradition of Pietro Lorenzetti celebrating military and political action, but here, raising it to the same rank as liturgical painting. Uccello's steeds are not just mounted animals but also the inevitable symbol of a caste and the tournaments in which—as in war—the manly virtues were forged. Knighthood survived the fiascos of Azincourt and Gallipoli in the form of rituals and as an eminent mode of action in everyday life. Of course one of the warriors is sporting a *mazzocchio*. The attention which Paolo Uccello lavished on objects did not however, lead to the first still lifes in Western painting: the first pictorial poets of the ordinary presence of objects came from the Flemish tradition. Those which litter the ground in the scene where Niccolo da Tolentino leads the Florentine army are disclosed in anything but a haphazard way: the broken and fallen lances and weapons create patterns of perpendiculars and parallels which structure space, and the obliques thus formed lead the eye of the spectator towards a vanishing point situated somewhere behind Niccolo da Tolentino's horse. Helmets and upturned shields complete this ordered array of military debris. In the foreground there is a war-club lying between the legs of the horses; the human figure has completely disappeared in its foreshortened armor. It is a faceless combat, in which only Niccolo da Tolentino and his groom, with faces uncovered, retain a semblance of humanity. But the way Paolo Uccello represents horses rearing up or in any other posture in the fray nuances even this touch of realism: the horses seem to have been modeled after those on merry-go-rounds, with distinctly colored hides of heraldic black, white, red and blue. While the

131

Opposite

PAOLO UCCELLO
**The Battle of San Romano:
Bernardino della Ciarda
Unhorsed** (detail)

shock of this mounted engagement would require a dynamic treatment, the horses all seem fixed and statuesque in their poses. The force lines across the three panels all converge on the impact of the lance on Bernardino della Ciarda's breastplate. Yet each composition stands on its own, with all of its elements unified, like the skyward pointing lances and flapping oriflammes, or the rhythmic patterns of legs–both mens' and horses'–in Micheletto da Cotignola's counter-attack battle though it may be, there is something monstrous about the whole thing. The masterfully rendered polished armor gleams in the crepuscular light; the helmets are plain or topped with fantastic crests, sealed to the outside except through the eye-slits of the visor. In this frightful melee, horses' heads and helmets seem to fuse into one form. Micheletto's action stands out from the shadows, bathed in an unreal light.

This use of lighting from unseen sources is not unlike what would be expected on the stage, and to be sure, Uccello's representation marshalls many accessories and devices from Florentine theater and feasts of the Renaissance. The *Battle of San Romano* depicts an imaginary world which challenges the eye to reconstruct the whole from the parts.

In this work, Paolo Uccello differentiated himself from the other painters of the Renaissance whose emphasis was the human figure. The men he represented all seem to bear the burden of nature, whether in the material sense as in the *Genesis* scenes of the Chiostro Verde, at the mercy of a cosmic cataclysm in *The Flood*, or as puppets on a stage in the Battle of San Romano.

In his last work, executed around 1465-1468, Uccello abandoned the grand scale of the *Battles* for a project of a more modest format. At the request of the Confraternity of the Holy Sacrament in Urbino, the artist left Florence to paint the predella for the altar of the church of Corpus Domini. His six panels depict the *Miracle of the Host*, treated in such a way as to attenuate the horror of the profanation without denying its tragic aspect. In the first episode, he creates dramatic tension by representing the host in a plain setting with a perspective treatment, a tiny cell of light against a dark background. The scenes are separated by the traditional medieval device of twisted columns, but what really distinguishes them from one another is their rational geometry and the various perspective effects. With their simplicity, the panels of the Urbino predella display the artist's concern for volume and the representation of reality.

The reaction of the Confraternity to this work remains a matter of conjecture. In any case, Uccello

PAOLO UCCELLO
The Battle of San Romano:
Niccolo da Tolentino Leading
the Florentines
1456, oil on wood,
182 x 320 cm.
National Gallery, London.

To illustrate this sequence of the
battle, Paolo Uccello used two
different perspective systems: with its
divisions and closures, the
background has a medieval
perspective, while the foreground is
handled in one-point perspective.

134

PAOLO UCCELLO
The Battle of San Romano:
Micheletto da Cotignola's
Counter-attack
1456, oil on wood,
180 x 315 cm.
Musée du Louvre, Paris.

In this, the decisive episode of the
battle, which may have occupied the
middle position in the original
arrangement in the Medici palace,
the artist used silver leaf to produce
effects of reflection and light.

PAOLO UCCELLO
**The Battle of San Romano:
Micheletto da Cotignola's
Counter-attack** (detail)

Above and opposite

PAOLO UCCELLO
**The Battle of San Romano:
Niccolo da Tolentino Leading
the Florentines**
(detail)

*Broken lances and a fallen knight in
armor have been treated as formal
patterns in strict perspective to
structure the stage-setting on which
the battle unfolds. The artist also
included many theatrical accessories of
his time.*

returned to the city on the Arno without having tackled the main panel of the altarpiece, a communion of the Apostles which was later executed by Justus of Ghent. It was in Florence that Paolo Uccello spent the last years of his life, until his death in 1475. Having been a child of the Late Gothic, he still nourished visions of chivalry. Having been schooled in the sculptural ideals of the time, he put a premium on vigorous modeling; fascinated by the perspective theories developed by Florentine artists, he inflected them according to optics of his own. In condensing elements from science, painting, and the inspiration of myth and fable, he combined the roles of scholar, painter and creator. In his *Imaginary Lives*, the writer Marcel Schwob compared the artist to an alchemist presiding over the fusion of metals to produce gold: "Uccello poured all forms into the crucible of form. He gathered them together, combined them. and melted them in order to transmute them into the single form which determined all the others. This is why Paolo lived like an alchemist ensconced in his house. He thought that he could transform all lines into a single ideal aspect. He wanted to envision the universe of creation as it was reflected in the eye of God, who sees all figures spring forth from a complex center." In 15th-century Tuscany however, Paolo Uccello was not the only alchemist enthralled by the play of vision and perspective problems.

Andrea del Castagno: master of line and relief

When Andrea del Castagno arrived in Florence in 1440, the painters of the time subscribed to one of two major tendencies. There were those like Fra Angelico and Filippo Lippi who concerned themselves with color and luminosity; while others concentrated their attention on line and plasticity of form. Andrea del Castagno, like Paolo Uccello, was among those who used light and shadow to create the impression of strong relief. His passage in Florence that year did not go unnoticed, for he was commissioned to paint portraits of the traitors of the Battle of Anghiari who were hanged from the windows of the Palazzo Podesta. The next two years found him in Venice working on frescoes for San Zaccharia which present formal qualities that seem to indicate the influence of Uccello and sculptural qualities that speak of Donatello.

The monumentality of his painting was given ample scope to display itself in the frescoes he executed on the walls of the Sant' Appolonia refectory between 1445 and 1450. His treatment of the Last Supper, with the disciples regularly disposed around the figure of

a

c

e

PAOLO UCCELLO
The Miracle of the Host
Former predella in six panels
from Justus de Ghent's altarpiece
in the Corpus Domini church in
Urbino.
1465-1469, wood,
32 x 343 cm.
Galleria Nazionale delle Marche,
Urbino.

b

d

f

a/ The sale of the consecrated host.
b/ The host thrown into the fire.
c/ The procession to preserve a particle of the host.
d/ The guilty woman is taken to the place of execution, while an angel appears.
e/ The usurer and his family are tied to the stake.
f/ Two angels and two demons fight over the woman's body before an altar.

Christ in a precisely-traced architectural setting as in the Renaissance spirit. The unity of the group and feeling of communion came not from the figures themselves, fairly individualized and uncouth, but rather from the overall compositional scheme: the perfectly ordered cenacle, whose tiled roof extends toward the viewer, and the white horizontal expanse of the table in the foreground which determines the alignment of the apostles.

Like Paolo Uccello and his constant research into optical effects, Andrea del Castagno strove no less tirelessly to create volume and lifelike bodies. Around 1450, in the great hall of the Villa Legnaia, he elaborated a new pictorial type that illustrated great figures of history and myth: three Florentine condottieri exalting their power and wit, the figure of *Pippo Spano* dominating also the picture space with his ferocity; the poets, represented by *Dante*, *Petrarch* and *Boccacio*, make show of more peaceful dispositions; the figures of the *Cumean Sybil*, *Esther* and the legendary *Tomyris* round off this iconographical program intended to celebrate both human dignity and heroic grandeur.

A contemporary critic, echoing Cristoforo Landiro, saw in Andrea del Castagno a "great master of drawing and relief." One year before dying of the plague in 1457, the artist gave a final demonstration of his talent in an illusionistic equestrian monument to Niccolo da Tolentino destined as a companion piece to the fresco of Sir John Hawkwood in the Cathedral of Florence. The dramatic intensity of his figures, though more harsh in feeling, make Andrea del Castagno a fitting heir to the great Masaccio.

Piero della Francesca:
The Story
of a Synthesis

Most of the issues which nourished controversy among artists in the Quattrocento merged into a masterful synthesis in the work of Piero della Francesca. Even the painter's story is exceptional for, like Leon Battista Alberti, he was born around 1420 not in Florence but in Borgo San Sepolcro, near Arezzo; a small Tuscan town to which he remained faithful until his death in 1492. Piero, however, did not confine himself to his home town but often travelled to ply his trade. In 1435 he was in Florence working with Domenico Veneziano on frescoes for Sant'Egidio (since destroyed). Between jobs at Arezzo and San Sepolcro, he was away on other commissions: at Ferrara to participate in the decoration of Lionello d'Este and Borso's castle, in Venice, and then in Rimini at mid-century. Apart from his stay in the city of the Doges, his trips coincided with those of Leon Battista Alberti. In Rimini, the architect converted the Franciscan church into a dynastic memorial at the behest of Sigismond Malatesta. There, Piero executed a fresco depicting the above-named lord kneeling before his tutelary saint. His fame spread so far that in 1459 he was called upon to decorate the private chamber of Pius II at the Vatican. According to Vasari, he also worked at Perugia, Ancona, Loretto and Pesaro. Of the many Italian cities in which he stayed during the course of his career, one stands out in particular: Urbino.

PIERO DELLA FRANCESCA
The Baptism of Christ
ca. 1465 tempera on wood,
167 x 116 cm.
National Gallery, London.

In the Baptism of Christ, *Piero della Francesca abandons the tradition of Masaccio and adopts a more serene rhythm that leads to a more complex spatial organization. There is not just space, but an airiness which gives a feeling of great depth.*

Opposite

PIERO DELLA FRANCESCA
The Baptism of Christ (detail)

It may be that in the humanistic atmosphere of this ducal city. which was graced with the first prince's palace of the Renaissance, he found a favorable environment and receptivity to his art. Among his works were a diptych devoted to Duke Federigo da Montefeltro, to whom he dedicated his *Treatise on Perspective*, while he dedicated a book on the geometry of regular bodies to his son, Guidobaldo.

Nothing is known of Piero della Francesca's first master, nor of the colleagues of his early career. How long had he been in Florence when he began to work with Domenico Veneziano? Did he already live in the vicinity of the city on the Arno? For certain, he had already seen the works of Masolino and Gentile da Fabriano and been drawn to the colors of Fra Angelico and Filippo Lippi. An avid reader of Alberti's treatise, he was equally fascinated by the works of Masaccio, the experiments of Brunelleschi, and the speculations of Uccello.

Birth and development of a personality

Before his crowning cycle, the *Legend of the True Cross*, executed for San Francesco's in Arezzo, his main achievements were the *Polyptych of Misericordia* of San Sepolcro, commissioned in 1445, the *Penitent Saint Jerome* from ca. 1450, and the *Portrait of Sigismond Malatesta* from the same period.

With his first polyptych, Piero della Francesca already asserted a powerful personality. The influence of Masaccio may be felt mostly in the general composition of the panels for, like Masaccio at the Carmine in Pisa, he used the theme of the Crucifixion as the climactic episode, all the while dramatizing the movement of the figures, and that of the *Virgin of Misericord*, but dominated by a new architectural vision. He went, however, far beyond his Florentine predecessors and the traditions expected by his patrons. The gold background and ultramarine-blue required by the contract were dispensed with in favor of a complete mastery of the moment and place. The figures inhabit an otherworldly space, beyond the realm of the material, subject only to the rule of light. The Virgin, majestically posed in the center, is the creation of a fundamentally new spirit. She unfurls her broad mantle in an ample gesture to form a sheltering niche for the group of faithful, yet her face expresses no trace of this action. Going beyond the hieratism of Byzantine or Gothic art, Piero brought into being a new type of figure which partakes neither of the historical, human or divine realms. This *Virgin of Misericord* stands in a world of Piero della Francesca's own making. The features of the face

are simple, the hairstyle unique, she stands statuefied by the architectonic folds of her dress and mantle, a pure creation of the artist's vision.

One outstanding feature of the polyptych is its background; for the first time in his career Piero dispensed with landscape and architecture. Yet, all the while complying with the Confraternity's request for gold, Piero asserted his complete originality, not to say singularity. The great simplicity which characterizes his work as a whole is already a feature of this polyptych. Piero reduces forms to their bare essentials. His figures are not decked out in the glamorous finery then in fashion, but are clothed in plain and often monochrome costumes. The stark simplicity that he obtains throughout rests upon geometric underpinnings. This is apparent in the figure of the Virgin, whose face is a perfect oval, the neck a cylinder, and the mantle and dress a series of parallel folds resting on the ground. Shown in frontal or profile views, his figures are literally regular bodies and obey the same theorems. Piero della Francesca went on to use geometry ever more consistently to construct his compositions. In the *Virgin of Hope*, the *Baptism of Christ*, or the *Madonna of Senigallia*, the main character occupies the middle of the picture, while the secondary figures are disclosed symmetrically on either side and on the same level. By such radical procedures, Piero created the conditions for solemnity, dignity and silence which compelled the spectator to contemplation. Piero used geometry not only as a framework for his compositions, but also as a foil for light; his forms all have very precise contours, and stand out all the more as his coloring did not follow the traditional shading patterns of the Quattrocento. The master from San Sepolcro alternated light and dark, warm and cool tones, with the rigor of a mathematician. His most perfect demonstration of this came at the church of San Francesco in Arezzo.

The Arezzo cycle

In his murals illustrating the *Legend of the True Cross*, Piero della Francesca brought his mastery of form and light to its peak. In answer to the prayers of one of the members of a noble family of Arezzo, Bicci di Lorenzo was commissioned to decorate the choir of the church of San Francesco. This Florentine painter died after having completed only a part, the arch of triumph with a *Last Judgement*, and Piero was entrusted with the rest of the program in 1452 or so. His beginnings with this project coincided with a change in the iconographic cycle: the theme

of the True Cross had already been treated by Agnolo Daddi in his decoration of the choir at Santa Croce in Florence at the end of the 14th century; Cenni di Francesco took it up again in 1410 in the Franciscan church in Volterra, and Masolino da Panicale in Empoli at San Stefano in 1424. The issue of the Cross was an important one for the popes at this time for they had to unify Christendom against the Ottoman threat and recapture Constantinople. Piero adopted this subject but differentiated himself from its previous illustrators by his choice of episodes, stressing certain scenes in particular and adding others. He drew his inspiration from liturgical texts, hymns, and *The Golden Legend*.

The cycle covers the three walls of the choir, beginning at the dawn of History with the *Death of Adam*, which is followed by another scene from the Old Testament, *The Queen of Sheba's visit to King Solomon*. Then come the *Dream of Constantine* and his *Defeat of Maxentius* and finally the *Battle between Heraclius and the King of Persia*, during which the True Cross was wrested from its ravishers and returned to Jerusalem. The artist's addition to the cycle was the New Testament scene of the *Annunciation* as counterpoint to Solomon. Unlike the other portrayers of this legend, Piero abandoned chronology the better to accentuate parallels between the subjects. On the right-hand wall of the choir the painter created a perfect geometric structure between the fresco panels: the tree which articulates the episode of the *Death of Adam* finds its correspondence in the column which separates the two scenes of the meeting of Solomon and the Queen of Sheba in the register below. The tree, a product of nature, has been transformed into a column, the work of man. There is an evident contrast between the bareness of the first mortals with their dramatic and fretful agitation, and the solemn court decor with its formal gestures and processions of figures midway between statue and column. The scene as a whole and its protagonists have all been treated as regular volumes subject to the laws of geometry. In the left half, the queen is still surrounded by nature's simplicity before her encounter with Solomon; on the right, however, we see Solomon's palace, a pure creation of Albertian architecture.

An unreal world

In addition to his total mastery of composition, Piero della Francesca worked with a great economy of means and knew how to use color and light as unifying elements. In *The Death of Adam* he deliberately limited his palette and opted for a monochrome handling, yet

Above and opposite

Piero della Francesca
The Resurrection
(detail of soldiers)

he succeeded in shading even these few colors into a vast range of delicate nuances. Piero was fond of alternating colors and knew how to bring out the value of each in relation to its chromatic context. Light was another of the means through which he defined form. Each figure was lit with the same intensity. Light enlivens the faces, accentuates the folds of the drapery and ornaments and emanates from the figures–yet there are no cast shadows. Piero's unreal world bathes in what could be called the principle of clear light. Only in the *Dream of Constantine* does he adhere to a form of luminism, but then it is to create an extraordinary vision. The way in which the artist carefully controlled the distribution of light or clarity enveloping figures and objects, one could think that he had looked to Flemish painting for his inspiration. Piero was the serene architect of light. The golden rays of the sun are reflected in the face of the *Madonna of Senigallia*, and this light spreads throughout the interior space, as in the works of the Dutch masters.

Piero repeated this achievement one last time around 1472, when he executed the portraits of the Duke of Urbino, Federigo da Montefeltro, and his wife, Battista Sforza. On the backs of the panels of the original diptych, Frederigo and Battista are depicted in triumph, solemnly enthroned, each upon a chariot, one drawn by unicorns and the other by white horses. The painter chose to set both the portraits and the chariots against landscape backgrounds that seem to stretch as far as the eye can see. Light from the sky filters gently over the faces and gives definition to their structure. Although giving only a profile view, the artist set down the most telling details and managed to express both the intelligence and strength of character of the duke surveying his domain.

In the *Madonna of Senigallia* (ca. 1470), with its play of light and shadow, and the *Nativity* from the same year, Piero della Francesca returned to his earlier pictorial language. But this Virgin, from the softness of her features, the warmth of her complexion, and the brightness of her gaze, would seem to live in the same world as ours. Like the Virgin, a native Tuscan adorned in the jewels of the Duchess of Urbino, the five musical angels of the *Nativity* all seem to have joined the species which they resemble. As beings shaped by light and dark, they herald the chiaroscuro works of Leonardo da Vinci, if not Jan Vermeer. Piero della Francesca had captured the Quattrocento eye as a wizard of geometry and abstraction; at the end of his career he cast his spell by integrating light into his painting and bringing life to his figures.

Above and opposite

PIERO DELLA FRANCESCA
Diptych of the Dukes of Urbino
(front: **Portrait of Battista Sforza**)
Tempera on wood. 47 x 33 cm.
Galleria degli Uffizi, Florence.

This likeness of Battista Sforza may have been executed posthumously. Note the complexity of the hair-do, which is composed of a jewel, a braid and a ribbon.

The Age
of Narration

Piero della Francesca's last passage in Florence came in 1440 or so. Not long after, in the 1460s and 1470s, the first generation of great innovators in art and architecture began to disappear. The city continued, however, to function as a thriving artistic center thanks to the activity of its many painters, whose prodigious output derived mainly from the tradition of the courtly novel. The narrative sense which appeared with Pesellino was developed in the works of Benozzo Gozzoli or Alesso Baldovinetti, and brought to its highest point in those of Domenico Ghirlandaio. In this area, which is so open to experimentation and innovation, yet so often marked by convention and academics, the work of Benozzo Gozzoli (1420-1497) stands out in particular for its originality.

Benozzo Gozzoli and the appeal of courtly art

Benozzo Gozzoli's apprenticeship was fully in keeping with the Quattrocento tradition. At the age of twenty he was already assisting Fra Angelico with his frescoes at San Marco and beginning further training as goldsmith with Ghiberti, then busy on the execution of his second Baptistery door. With the former he also worked at the Cathedral of Orvieto and collaborated on the decoration of the chapel of

BENOZZO GOZZOLI
The Procession of the Magi
(detail with portrait of the Emperor John VIII Paleologus)
1459, fresco.
Palazzo Medici-Ricardi, Florence.

For this representation of Emperor John VIII Paleologus as one of the Three Wise Men, Gozzoli based his work on a medallion designed by Pisano in 1438. However, he made the face younger and replaced the traditional and unwieldy Byzantine tiara with a crown resting on a peacock-plumed velvet cap.

Nicolas V at the Vatican. Fascinated by Fra Angelico's spirituality, and adopting his delicate color-schemes, he indulged in marvellous visions, yet closer to the spectator because he transposed them into contemporary terms by including details from everyday life. The quality of his composition in *The Distribution of Alms* in the Vatican chapel demonstrates his mastery of perspective. This talent as a storyteller is plain to see in his frescoes of the *Legend of Saint Francis* at Montefalco. and his reputation as a decorator spread so far that he was given commissions in Viterbo and San Gimignano. While, in the eyes of his fellow artists, Gozzoli appeared more of a minor master, Vasari, impressed by his abundant production, wrote that "he outdid his contemporaries by the quantity of his works, such that, among them, there had to be some of quality!"

Gozzoli's renown reached its peak when he was asked to decorate the private chapel of the Medici Palace in Florence at the behest of Piero, who passed over Paolo Uccello, Filippo Lippi and Domenico Veneziano in his favor.

It may be that, as their correspondence shows, Benozzo Gozzoli proved to be more accommodating of his patron's wishes and thus tilted the scales. Be that as it may, he executed a series of frescoes that included *The Nativity* and, as the main piece, a *Procession of the Three Kings* which he set in a fairytale landscape that has something of the gardens of Paradise. Gozzoli's work was in fact a display of Medici power, for the Oecumenical Council had just transferred Ferrara into Florentine tutelage. The Magi are represented with the features of John Paleologus, the Patriarch of Constantinople and Lorenzo de' Medici. Their brilliant suite is composed of various princes, political allies and humanists connected with the family, and both the costumes of the pages and ornaments of the horses proudly sport the Medici coat-of-arms. In a setting which partakes both of Eden and of the Tuscan countryside, Benozzo Gozzoli has transposed a biblical episode into the contemporary Quattrocento context for the greater glory of the ruling house. In order to depict this state of grace, Gozzoli marshalled the means of courtly art, here destined for consumption by the *haute-bourgeoisie*. The frescoes have been treated not unlike tapestries; landscapes take up a great deal of the pictorial space and are replete with picturesque details and all manner of richly adornments. As in the frescoes of San Gimignano and of the Camposanto in Pisa, the artist made full use of the artistic means at his disposal to achieve effects which may seem facile, but that are nonetheless full of freshness and elegance. His art is a holdover from the miniatures that were in fashion at the turn of the century.

BENOZZO GOZZOLI
The Procession of the Magi
(detail of right wall)

*The youngest of the Magi was given
the likeness of Lorenzo the
Magnificent, then eleven or twelve
years old. He is at the head of a
cortege which includes Cosimo de'
Medici, Piero the Lame and his
brother Giuliano.*

161

The tendencies so strongly asserted by the previous generation of Florentine painting were now being expressed in a more nuanced manner. The painters of the 1460s and 70s could explore both line and color. This was the case of Alesso Baldovinetti, whose debt to his master, Domenico Veneziano, is visible in his serene compositions filled with light, and who owed his sense of volume and firm outline to Uccello and Castagno. The decoration for the chapel of the Cardinal of Portugal at San Miniato, executed between 1466 and 1473, grew out of these twofold roots. When he painted his *Annunciation*, Baldovinetti looked to the example of Domenico Veneziano for his lighting of the face of the Virgin. But he had Castagno in mind when it came to handling the sharp silhouettes and expressive intensity of his figures of *Prophets* and *Evangelists*.

The serenity of his color-schemes reappears in the *Madonna* of 1450. Yet in this last work, as in his *Nativity* for the cloister of Santa Annunziata, Baldovinetti ushered in a new direction in Florentine painting. Like Antonio del Pollaiuolo, he integrated landscape in the most natural way. Vasari writes that "he was fond of making landscapes and copied them from life, exactly as they were." The grand vista of the Arno valley stretching behind the Madonna in the Flemish manner were the fruit of diligent and direct study, which a painter like Pollaiuolo took to its extreme in harmonizing both figure and landscape.

The interest of this new generation of painters for the narrative tradition and the Flemish manner found its finest expression in the art of Domenico Ghirlandaio (1449-1494). His first works owe something to Verrocchio—who also worked with Baldovinetti. Later he would combine the luminosity so dear to his master with a more gentle treatment of religious subjects. eclectic in his tastes, he found the impetus toward more realism in the Portinari triptych by Hugo van der Goes, which arrived in 1482. His vast and balanced mural compositions often make use of architectural element. The prime example of this is in his frescoes representing the *Life of Saint John the Baptist* executed in Santa Maria Novella between 1485 and 1490. Ghirlandaio set the scenes in front porticoes with arcades, apse-like spaces, interiors defined by cornices and coffered ceilings in perspective, campaniles, or simply walls, or in the midst of landscapes with antique buildings. All these staircases, porticoes, arcades and colonnades were the pictorial offsprings of Brunelleschi's architecture and were expressly mentioned in the contracts between patron and painter. The contract for the frescoes in Santa Maria Novella passed in 1485 with the Tornabuoni family, stimulated the

BENOZZO GOZZOLI
The Procession of the Magi
(detail with Emperor John VIII
Paleologus on his horse)

Opposite

BENOZZO GOZZOLI
The Procession of the Magi
(detail with the Emperor's pages)

*Behind the mounted Wise Men in
ceremonial dress come the young
pages and attendants on foot, dressed
in costumes of fitting elegance.*

BENOZZO GOZZOLI
The Procession of the Magi
(details)

*Most of the figures were painted from
live models and given the likeness of
Gozzoli's contemporaries.*

Opposite

BENOZZO GOZZOLI
The Procession of the Magi
(detail with Joseph, Patriarch of
Constantinople)

167

BENOZZO GOZZOLI
The Procession of the Magi
(detail)

*After the Medici, the painter tried to
represent as many likenesses as
possible, often without concern for the
actual space taken up by the body;
only a few figures enjoy sufficient
space.*

Opposite

The Procession of the Magi
(detail)
Benozzo Gozzoli's self-portrait is
indicated by an inscription on his
hat.

169

inclusion of "figures, houses, castles, cities, mountains, and birds and animals of all kinds." A master of the fresco, Ghirlandaio, like Gozzoli, integrated into his biblical scenes the faithful likenesses of real people–an excellent way of pleasing patrons. His workshop was prosperous and could boast the presence of the young Michelangelo in 1488. His impeccable style displayed both an elegant distinction and a certain aloofness. Ghirlandaio succeeded in reconciling two distant worlds: that of the Bible and that of the Renaissance. In his *Visitation*, which features views of both Florence and Rome, he brought Antiquity and Christianity together.

In *The Angel appears to Zaccharias*, in addition to the portraits of the Tornabuonis, Marsilio Ficino and his humanist disciples Politian and Cristoforo Landino, there is an inscription in praise of Florentine prosperity: "The year 1490, when the fairest of cities, famous for its riches, its victories, its arts and its monuments, enjoyed the sweetness of abundance, health and peace."

Under the rule of Lorenzo the Magnificent, Florence was considered the capital of the West. It was then that Ghirlandaio painted the frescoes which dazzled the nobles, charmed ambassadors, and left us the image of a brilliant culture. After seeing the frescoes of Gozzoli, the poet Rainer Maria Rilke was inspired to write: "The time was an especially favorable one for feasts. It is enough to gaze upon their likenesses to see how well these people felt in the midst of joy and feasting decked in their finery and adornments without wan vanity as if it were completely natural, a symbol of the luxurious magnificence which they discovered a bit more each year, yet more boldly within themselves."

Painting

and

Poetry

*I*n their diversity and singularity, the works of Paolo Uccello, Piero della Francesca, and the narrative painters show the wealth of new directions explored by the Quattrocento painters. During the decades around the middle of the century, the diversity of styles was equalled only by the proliferation of new talent. Although mainstream art drew upon theories of painting with all their rules and principles, the individual artists manifested originality in their works anyway. The program elaborated by Alberti in his famous treatise from 1436 showed painters the way to the organization of space. Draughtsmen like Uccello and Castagno devoted their energy to geometric systematization and, especially, to perspective construction. Filippo Lippi brought his sense of color to bear on pictorial composition, a register which found its finest expression in the work of Sandro Botticelli at the end of the century.

Filippo Lippi and the birth of lyricism

Like Fra Angelico, the painter Filippo Lippi (1406-1469) also donned the monk's robe, but, unlike his more beatific brother, it seems not to have been less from personal vocation than from obedience to his father, who put him in the Carmel monastery in Florence. Lippi was only

Opposite

SANDRO BOTTICELLI
Primavera
(detail of Venus)
1477-1488, tempera on wood,
203 x 314 cm.
Galleria degli Uffizi, Florence.

173

fifteen years old when he took his vows, and, although he left the monastery ten years later he remained a monk. After working in Padua, he returned to Florence in 1437, yet he never undertook the cloistered life of the Order again, but became a lay monk and established his own studio. His reputation was already fairly widespread and he was never short of admirers. His unconventional life, however, often brought him into conflict with the religious and municipal authorities. This did not prevent him from being appointed chaplain at the convent of Santa Margherita in Prato, nor from eloping with one of the nuns, Lucrezia Buti, who may also have been his model! This liaison led to the birth of a son, Filippino, in 1457 who followed in his father's—and especially Botticelli's—footsteps to become one of the great painters of the late Quattrocento. Thanks to the intercession of Cosimo de' Medici, the Pope relieved Filippo and Lucrezia of their vows in 1461 and permitted them to marry at last.

This tumultuous life does not seem to have been an obstacle to Lippi's career as a painter; yet many questions remain unanswered. With whom did he apprentice when he left the monastery? What kind of training did he receive and where? In all likelihood he benefited from the instruction of Lorenzo Monaco, but the most decisive impetus must have come from the Brancacci chapel, in his own monastery, where Masaccio was at work in 1426. Lippi's first works—*The Confirmation of the Rules of the Order* (1432, Carmine church) and the *Madonna of Humility* (1434, Sforza castle in Milan)—show clearly that he had opted for realism in his simplification of forms and somewhat naive coarseness.

Around 1437, however, under the influence of Fra Angelico, Filippo Lippi made efforts to smooth out the rough edges and introduce more delicacy. This new direction is perceptible in a work like the *Madonna of Tarquinia*. Taking his cue from the colorist tradition, he worked out original solutions to pictorial problems along the way. His encounter with Angelico attenuates the harsh elasticity that he had inherited from Masaccio. Lippi asserted his own specific style in his new approach to light and lighting. In his *Coronation of the Virgin* (1441-1447), executed for the San Ambrogio church in Florence, he distributed a wide variety of objects and dynamic forms in a discontinuous space; yet the quality of the details, the chromatic diversity and the subtle handling of the paint dematerializes the composition and create an extraordinary softness. Filippo Lippi manages in this way to wed the vibrancy of light with the melodiousness of line. This sensitivity to linear rhythms and talent for coloring produced elegant silhouettes and

delicate color harmonies which endow works like the 1450 *Annunciation*, the *Adoration in the forest* (1458-1460), and especially the *Madonna and Child with two angels* with a poetic atmosphere of great beauty.

By developing melodious line and color-schemes, Lippi definitively evolved away from the burly figures and constructions of Masaccio. Libertine though he may have been, the renegade friar continued to treat only religious subjects in his frescoes or panels. Structural forms à-la-Brunelleschi reappear in his *Annunciation*, but he attenuates them by his use of color and the attitudes of the figures. In his *Adoration in the Forest*, he combined narration and imagination to accede to fantasy; but he dispensed with real space in the frescoes painted between 1456 and 1466 for the Cathedral of Prato by reproducing this atmosphere and diaphanous luminosity to envelop his *Saint John the Baptist in the Desert*. Only his *Funerary Mass for Saint Stephen*—in the same cathedral—retains a rational organization of space and majestically posed figures, as in a last homage to the Masaccio of the Brancacci Chapel.

Filippo Lippi's graceful and serene figures, posed in charming attitudes, and the subdued richness of his coloring, created a lyrical vein which his son, Filippino, and Botticelli both tapped during the second half of the Quattrocento. His contemporary. Cristoforo Landino, formulated his praise in these terms: "he painted with grace and adornment; he had extraordinary skill and was excellent in everything that concerned composition, variety color, relief and also all manner of ornamentation." Among the pupils of the ex-friar was a young man who was destined to become the greatest Florentine painter of the last years of this "golden century" so admirably evoked by Vasari in the first lines of his biography of the artist.

Botticelli, apprentice goldsmith

Alessandro di Mariano di Vanni Filipepi was born in Florence in 1445, at a time when the city on the Arno was being embellished with new churches and palaces and works of art by creators of the highest caliber. Under the direction of Michelozzo, the Medici palace commissioned by Cosimo was rising above its foundations while the versatile architect was also rebuilding the monastery of San Marco, where Fra Angelico was busy putting up a testimony of his faith and skill. The beginning of work at Santo Spirito under Brunelleschi's direction, one year before his death, was the last testament of the man whose name and example resound

throughout the Renaissance. Especially busy then were the masters of the line; Andrea del Castagno was at work on the frescoes for Sant' Apollonia, while Paolo Uccello was hard at play with perspective schemes and optical illusions in his scenes of the *Life of Noah* at the Chiostro Verde in Santa Maria Novella.

The social milieu in which Alessandro spent the early years of his life was far removed from that of the masters who enjoyed the protection of the Medici and their privileged pupils. His father was a modest tanner in the Ognissanti quarter, whose textile and leather workers spread the fame of Florentine crafts as far as Northern Europe. But the workers of the right bank of the Arno were in constant contact with craftsmen of all kinds thanks to the construction and decoration projects which brought them together.

In his biography, Vasari tells us that Botticelli "learned only what he liked, but refused to apply himself in reading, writing and arithmetic." An unwilling student, the young Alessandro was apprenticed to a goldsmith by his father.

It was perhaps during this training that Botticelli acquired his taste for the precise, incised line which characterized his painting. It was also during this period that he decided to become a painter. In 1464 he was admitted into Filippo Lippi's workshop, where he remained until 1467 and changed his name to the simpler and more melodious-sounding Sandro Botticelli. We have no way of identifying the works he executed while under contract with his master, but the sensuality of Filippo Lippi is apparent in his first *Madonnas*, considered to be studio works. He seems to have been influenced also by the school of Verrocchio and had affinities with the style of Pollaiuolo. Workshops specializing in both painting and sculpture were in their heyday then and very much in demand. Piero del Pollaiuolo was commissioned by the merchants' guild to execute a series of seven paintings for their council room, but through the intercession of Tomaso Solderini, an agent close to the Medici, he was obliged to turn the theme of *Force* over to Botticelli in 1479. It was in that year, therefore, that the youthful master set his own studio up in the family house of the Borgo Ognissanti amidst the clatter and vibrations of their weaver neighbor's looms. In 1472 he was listed as a member of the guild of San Luca and recorded as working already with Filippino Lippi. His reputation soon spread beyond his native city, and for a while it seemed as if he would be entrusted with fresco work at the Camposanto, but the commission never materialized, and Botticelli returned to Florence beset with other orders. At the

SANDRO BOTTICELLI
Primavera
1477-1488, tempera on wood,
203 x 314 cm.
Galleria degli Uffizi, Florence.

*From left to right: Mercury
dispersing clouds, the Three Graces,
Venus and Cupid loosing an arrow,
Spring, Flora pursued by Zephyr .*

SANDRO BOTTICELLI
Primavera
(detail of the figure of Spring)

Opposite

SANDRO BOTTICELLI
Primavera
(detail of the figure of Spring)

request of the banker Zanobi del Lama, he painted an *Adoration of the Magi* in 1475 for Santa Maria Novella, one of his undisputed masterpieces.

When Florence was torn by factional strife between the great rival families, Botticelli's ties with the Medici were further strengthened and he became an intimate member of their circle of protégés. After the events of the Pazzi conspiracy which led to the assassination of Giuliano de' Medici in 1478, he was entrusted with the task of painting the conspirators hung at the windows of the Palazzo Vecchio. His style had attained full maturity by then, and no doubt at the behest of Lorenzo di Pierfrancesco, a rich cousin of Lorenzo the Magnificent, he painted the first of his great mythological compositions, *Primavera*, or Spring.

Pope Sixtus IV called him then to Rome to work on the Sistine Chapel, a project which brought together the greatest painters of the day. Along with Perugino, Cosimo Roselli, Domenico Ghirlandaio and later, Luca Signorelli, he collaborated on an iconographic program intended to establish parallels between the lives of Christ and Moses. In 1481, he was given three frescoes to paint depicting *The Youth of Moses*, the *Punishment of the Levites*, the *Temptation of Christ* and the *Sacrifice and Purification of the Leper*. The generosity of his retribution was a measure of the Pope's admiration for his work. His sojourn in the Vatican did not affect his style, but he left with a solid reputation as a fresco painter.

His return to Florence coincided with Leonardo da Vinci's departure for Milan. As one of the most prestigious artists of his time, Botticelli attracted many pupils to his studio, which began to specialize in the production of Madonnas, devotional paintings, coffers and portraits in answer to a correspondingly increasing demand. With the Pollaiuolo brothers away in Rome and Verrocchio in Venice to execute the Colleoni monument, Botticelli had little competition to worry about; yet he and his three assistants never tired in exercising their wit in the conception or realization of their works—which they signed in original ways—or of resorting to guile in order to sell them.

This was also the period of the great mythological piece. The allegorical scenes painted for the walls of Villa Lemmi around 1480 still display the freshness of *Primavera*. After *Mars and Venus* in 1483, he painted *Pallas and the Centaur* in the same year, then the *Birth of Venus* in 1484, all the while devoting time to religious subjects. His illustration of Neoplatonic themes did not prevent him from returning to this sphere of imagery, especially as Florence was

undergoing reform at the prompting of Savonarola, the prior of San Marco. His incendiary preaching, dramatic anathemas against corruption, and apocalyptic prophecies announcing the imminent downfall of the city were intended to overhaul the moral and religious life of the Florentines. The upheavals caused by the preacher and his execution and the Medici's flight in 1494 must have severely shaken up Botticelli's poetic world view leaving him alone, face to face with his own anguish. After the loss of Savonarola and his protectors, he succumbed to a mystical crisis out of which came the grief-ridden Pieta of the *Entombment* (1495) and the vision of the *Allegorical Crucifixion* (1500-1505).

His spiritual conflicts also rang the knell of his career as an artist. Between 1503 and 1505 he was unable to pay his dues to the painters' guild, the flow of commission began to dry, and while he sat on the committee which decided on the placement for Michelangelo's *David*, this was mainly an honorific position. Left at the wayside of the new artistic tendencies in Florence, which had been won over to the ideas and works of Leonardo da Vinci—who returned in 1500—and Michelangelo, withdrawn into an archaic style that could not withstand the competition of their new approaches, Botticelli died almost forgotten in 1510, having ridden the Wheel of Fortune full circle.

A master of color and line

Stylistically, Botticelli's work is in the direct line of Filippo Lippi's, with its precisely contoured figures, luminous flesh-tones and lively color-schemes. These qualities enabled him to excel in portraiture as well. A comparison between the *Madonnas* of the master and the early *Virgins* of his pupil shows an astonishingly similarity in the compositions with their harmonious and colorful forms. The works of Lippi and Botticelli are at the antipodes of the severe plasticity of Masaccio. Standing removed from the historical stage of the Brancacci Chapel and from the religious sphere of Fra Angelico, Botticelli turned his attention to the more natural features of the human figures, giving emphasis to feeling and the softness characteristic of Lippi. Yet he took the figures of his master one step further, so to speak, and turned their poses almost into a dance. Their expressions and gestures transpose the religious scenes into a poetic register. The faces of his *Virgins*, whose beauty is none other than the beauty of a real woman, are all tinged with melancholy. Botticelli did not consider classical Antiquity as an authoritative source. The realm of an imagined perfection, it was an ideal, a myth which

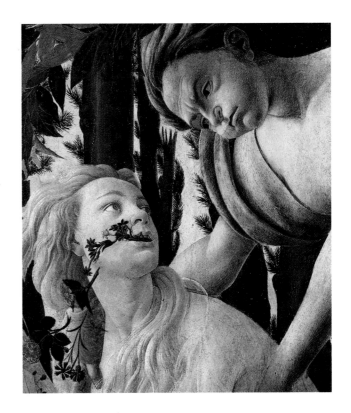

SANDRO BOTTICELLI
Primavera
(detail of Flora and Zephyr)

Opposite

SANDRO BOTTICELLI
Primavera
(detail of the Three Graces)

183

could be combined with profane and biblical history. Thus Christ could be seen as an avatar of Apollo and Orpheus, and the Virgin as a new persona for Diana or Venus. Even when there is a hint of the influence of Verrocchio or of Pollaiuolo, as in the firm modeling of the face of *Fortezza*, or Strength, there is still something indolent and dreamy about the figure. Line, which became the backbone of naturalism in Antonio and Piero del Pollaiuolo, is lighter in Botticelli and has a poetic freedom which was expressed even in his early *Madonnas*.

Botticelli's work marks further a spectacular break in the alliance between art and science championed by the first great masters of the Renaissance and which found its highest expression in Piero della Francesca. It came at a critical time when the main systems of figuration, perspective and conception of space were being questioned. Composition, for Botticelli, did not gravitate around perspective alone. He did not violate its principles, but never made it the crux of his spatial constructions; it was even a device he used to isolate figures and objects, to put distance between them.

In his *Birth of Venus*, the waves and shore are completely incidental to the main figure, standing in its splendid nudity and solitude, while in *Primavera* the flower-dotted field has no depth whatsoever. Space in Botticelli is more of an image, or symbol of reality, than its literal representation. For the master from Borgo Ognissanti, a picture was a pure abstraction, and this is precisely what made it beautiful. Even line was not a predictable element: it rises rapidly here, falls there, joins then disjoins, falling apart before recombining. The sudden linear disjunctions neutralize all feeling of movement and tends to abolish the physical meaning of the image.

For the sake of the unity of the image, the artist consistently sacrificed composition. In a painting like the 1475 *Adoration of the Magi* the broken arches of ancient Roman inspiration have been reduced to mere accessories, while the landscape is practically non-existent. The peacock standing on the wall is a sign pointing to the Orient. The scene, in which Cosimo de' Medici has been cast as one of the kings and other figures from his entourage as worshippers of the Virgin and Child, is pure theater. The ruins, rocks and wooden architecture represent the forces of nature, the grandeur of poverty and the rebirth of culture. Each element has a specific symbolic charge.

In his treatment of the four *Adoration of the Magi* which he painted between 1470 and 1475, which transform the sacred event into a worldly get-together, Botticelli drew on the Florentine tradition represented by

SANDRO BOTTICELLI
The Birth of Venus
(details)

Masterfully rendered by a V-shaped
stroke, the waves of the sea which
forms the background of the mythical
Birth of Venus, *graced with flying*
rose blossoms, transpose the scene
into the realm of pure symbol.

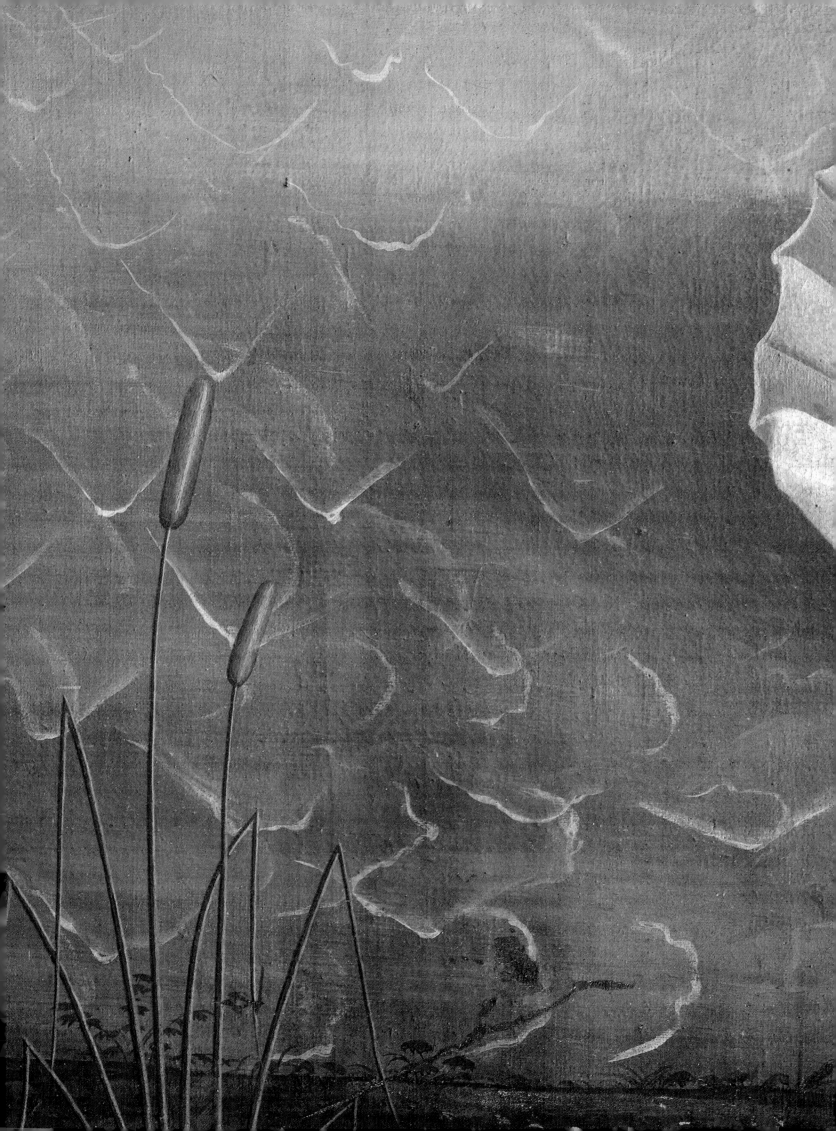

Lorenzo Monaco. If the theme of the Epiphany was so popular among the bourgeoisie of Florence, it was because it suggested better than any other theme the divine mercy that awaited those who, like the powerful kings paying homage to the humble Infant, devoted a part of their riches to the service and glory of the Church. Botticelli thus transformed the Adoration of the Magi into an apotheosis of the Medici and their court, arrayed in their most festive attire before the broken-down stable which houses the manger and other solemn evocations. The scene is an accumulation of fictions.

The colors, too, contribute to this effect, exploding into brilliance at one point only to fade away without leaving so much as a glow behind. They are incarnations of the golden light of the sun, and indeed, they are sometimes broken down into particles of gold. The picture as a whole, being an assemblage of discreet parts, eludes any clear definition: who can say whether the diaphanous veils of the three Graces in *Primavera* are meant to cover or discover their nudity? Is it the play of fabrics that creates movement or does the dance originate in the bodies? If anything, this trio of beauties is draped in air. Flora, wrapped in her dress, is woman, goddess and garden all at once. Whether the diadems and necklaces be of gold or of flowers, their metaphoric and metamorphic value remains the same. These images transcend their reality and their physical substance to become transmuted into pure beauty, beyond time and space.

The great mythological compositions

Botticelli was fond of painting the allegorical subjects so dear to the intellectual elite at the Medici court. He followed Alberti's theories of Vision to a great extent, but strove above all to reconcile these basic principles with humanistic culture which, at this late Quattrocento stage, was more interested in poetic discourse for its own sake rather than that of moral edification or historical example. Painting, for Botticelli, was related to poetry. His images are abundant, polyvalent, ambiguous, full of allegorical meanings and enigmas, and always have a potential for transformation. The main figure in *Primavera* is a quotation of the Virgin in Baldovinetti's *Annunciation*. Sacred images veer towards the profane, if not allegoric. The masterpieces which he executed for the Medici where born of this vision of art in which poetry and painting are one.

Botticelli's *Primavera* is a direct projection of the reign of Venus from the texts of Politian, which evoke "a realm which is the abode of grace; in which the lascivious

SANDRO BOTTICELLI
The Birth of Venus
1484, tempera and oil,
172 x 278 cm.
Galleria degli Uffizi, Florence .
Along with Primavera *and* Pallas
and the Centaur, *the* Birth of
Venus *was the third of Botticelli's
major mythological compositions.
Here he opted for simplicity and
followed Politian's* Stanzas *which
exalt art and life.*

Opposite

SANDRO BOTTICELLI
The Birth of Venus
(detail)

190

Zephyr wings in pursuit of Flora, and the green meadows are a-bloom." He painted a dream garden filled, like a medieval tapestry, with all sorts of flowers native to the Tuscan countryside, while rhythmic figures go through the graces of a ritual choreography. The eye is struck at first glance by the gracious forms and luxuriant vegetation described in harmonious colors and flowing lines. Yet for all the light, the scene is set in a twilight world. The figures themselves seeming to float above the ground, itself only a verdant carpet without depth, reinforce this feeling of evanescence. Botticelli's picture is an initiation into Neoplatonic imagery: Venus, symbolizing Love which rules the world, is shown between Mercury parting the clouds, the three dancing Graces, Spring sowing flowers, and Flora fleeing before Zephyr. The composition however has less to do with knowledge than with poetry. Placed at a remove from the others, the main figure stands between groups serving as veritable stanzas in the melodic flow of a splendid poem. Even the parallels of the tree trunks and the silhouetted foliage participate in this stately rhythm. They are interrupted only long enough to accommodate the figure of Venus in an aureola-shaped bower. Botticelli depicts the magical merging of nature with the human as well as of the human with nature.

In the *Birth of Venus,* his second major composition for the Medici, the artist opted for simplicity, reducing the number of figures in order to highlight the symbol. It is his hymn to Woman no longer cast in the role of the Virgin. In this Botticelli closely follows the *Stanzas* of Politian, who praises the triumph of life and exalts the work of art. Like Pallas, Venus' charm is all in her gracious form and cascading blond hair. This image recalls the words of Alberti written four decades before: "I like to see hair... curled into spirals, almost into knots, waving in the wind, reminding one of flames intertwined like snakes, now rising together, now falling away." Yet Pallas, with her gown and cloak, displays more substance than Venus who, despite her covering of flesh, verges on transparency. Each element of the picture is poised on the edge of the non-material. The comma-shapes rendering the waves transforming the sea into pure symbol.

Executed after the Sistine frescoes in Rome, the *Birth of Venus* indicates a return to the Neoplatonic inspiration of the Medici circle. Botticelli's sources for *Primavera* were the allegorical scenes painted in Villa Lemmi, yet no one ever took Neoplatonism so far as he did. In depicting a young man introduced into the circle of the Liberal Arts and a young woman endowed with gifts from Venus and the Graces, he created scenes of extraordinary poetic impact. The subtle color harmonies and the pervasive atmosphere of grace seem no

SANDRO BOTTICELLI
The Birth of Venus
(detail)

*Amid a hail of rose blossoms, a pair
of wind divinities blow Venus
towards shore where a Nymph waits
to cover her in a flowery mantle.*

193

longer to have anything to do with light or space.

In these frescoes, the painter produced images that break away from sensible reality. As Rainer Maria Rilke put it: "Botticelli's figures pass through the world without touching it, the mute recipients of a star which they can disclose to no one."

Savonarola's harangues against the Neoplatonists led Botticelli to abandon his ambitious mythological subject in favor of a more religious, not to say pious, production. But he took up a literary theme one last time in 1495, transforming the classical text written by Lucian in front of a painting by Apelles. In his *Calumny of Apelles*, Botticelli gave a magnificent demonstration of the extent of his humanist culture and formulated his scientific vision of painting. Well-acquainted with the theoretical texts, he laid down a perfectly orthodox perspective construction for the scene. Having studied each movement in detail, he drew the figures with a great purity of line. With its friezes, statues, coffers and allegorical bas-reliefs, the architectural setting creates a very solemn and serene atmosphere. The figures in front of this decor, however, are in the grips of a dramatic frenzy. Thrice interrupted by dark figures, the movement resumes with renewed violence in a repetitive scansion. The harshness of the color and the conventional treatment of the light serve to heighten the abstract quality of the scene.

The momentum generated in this severe and tragic work was unfortunately not transmitted to the compositions of his last years. Botticelli even abandoned the perspective so dear to the Renaissance masters and reverted to a medieval archaism, which he took to the extreme in his *Mystic Nativity* dated around 1500. The signatory inscription, which includes a text in Greek, makes explicit reference to the spiritual climate in which this work was created: "This picture was painted by me, Sandro, at the end of the year, during the disorders in Italy, in the middle of the time after the time, according to Chapter II of St. John, during the second scourge of the Apocalypse, when Satan was loosed upon the world for three and a half years." His last works attained new heights of spiritual exaltation. Like Fra Angelico at San Marco, Botticelli took up the great themes of Church history and its edifying visions, but where the representations depicted by the blessed friar derived from religious certainty, those of his successor are wracked by an anguished and tragic tension which strikes to the heart of faith itself.

Opposite

SANDRO BOTTICELLI
The Calumny of Apelles
(detail)

Inspired by Savonarola's preaching, Botticelli evolved in the last years of the 15th century towards a severe style imbued with spirituality. In depicting the theme of the Calumny of Apelles, he wanted to show the beauty of truth next to the horror of lies and the precariousness of human judgement.

Directly related to his work are the charming female figures painted by his student Filippino Lippi (1457-1504). Like his master, Filippino broke away from the constraints of linear perspective, tailoring the size of his figures in proportion to their importance, but he went to greater extremes in the cult of the line and drawing, which often becomes nervous and choppy. Commissioned in 1484 to complete the frescoes left unfinished by Masolino and Masaccio at the Brancacci Chapel, he made efforts to adapt his style to that of his great predecessors. During this same period however, he surpassed Botticelli in his delicacy and aetheticism, accentuating in the two *tondi* of his *Annunciation* the expressive folds of the costumes and filling the space with decorative objects of all kinds. His figures have the candour of the *Virgins* in which his master had excelled, but the busy decor and profusion of ornament were of his own production. At the Carafa Chapel in Rome (1489-1490), or in his scenes from the *Lives of Saint John and Saint Philip* in the Strozzi Chapel at Santa Maria Novella (1498-1502), he gave free rein to his own temperament, characterized by a strict line, a romantic sense of history and, as Vasari noted, a fascination for vestiges from the antique and "bizarre ornaments." With Filippino Lippi, the great force field of the Florentine Renaissance came to an end.

SANDRO BOTTICELLI
The Calumny of Apelles
1495, tempera on wood,
62 x 91 cm.
Galleria degli Uffizi, Florence.

*Like a marvel out of Antiquity, the
decor of the Calumny displays a
serene formality. Botticelli rendered
the architectural setting in great
detail, presenting allegorical and
moral allegories in the reliefs, statues,
friezes and coffers to the
contemplation of the spectator. In
front of this decor evocative of
wisdom and its limits, he disposed
his figures in a rush of motion
interrupted three times by a dark
accent. The drawing of the poses and
gestures is of a great purity.*

197

SANDRO BOTTICELLI
The Calumny of Apelles
(detail)

*Starting at the feet of the victim
dragged by the hair, the violent
movement culminates in the throne of
the ill-advised judge and is channeled
back again by the outstretched arm.
The judge, personified by King
Midas with donkeys' ears, is seated
between Suspicion and Ignorance,
and holds his hand out to Rancour
guiding Calumny.*

198

Verrocchio and his studio

During the period between 1465 and 1480, artistic activity in Florence was dominated by two major studios. The first was headed by Piero and Antonio del Pollaiuolo, whose works are easy to confuse. Antonio, skilled painter, sculptor, goldsmith and engraver, executed portraits, medallions and statues for the Medici and other wealthy Florentine families, also frescoes and embroidery designs for the churches, and even tombs for the popes. Influenced by Donatello and Castagno, his chief concerns were the expression of physical effort and the depiction of movement. His treatment of modeling was precise, as was his handling of styling bodies, of which he seems to have been especially fond, along with angular poses. He seems to have been attentive also to Flemish painting for the backgrounds of his compositions are often occupied by vast landscapes stretching out to the horizon. Around 1489, according to Lorenzo de' Medici, he was considered "the leading master in the city and, some enlightened connoisseurs say, no doubt the best who ever existed."

The second studio which profoundly determined artistic practice at this time was directed by Verrocchio (1435-1488). Born Andrea di Cione, he owed his surname to his first master, the goldsmith Giuliano Verrocchio, a custom then still in use. He started out working in Donatello's studio and soon became the official sculptor of the

ANDREA DEL VERROCCHIO
David
(entire and detail)
ca. 1476, bronze, 125 cm.
Museo Nazionale (Bargello),
Florence.

*The elegantly-attired David by
Verrocchio is the opposite of the
nude, sensual and vulnerable David
of Donatello. Holding a sword in
one hand and resting his other hand
brazenly on his hip, he dominates
the head of Goliath and shares his
triumph with the spectator.*

Medici for whom he executed, in 1472, the tomb of *Pietro and Giovanni de' Medici*, a sarcophagus made of bronze and porphyry. Following in Donatello's footsteps, he took up one of his most famous motifs and made his own bronze version of *David* in 1476. Three years later. he produced the *Winged Genie* which may be seen today on the fountain of the Palazzo Vecchio.

The 1470s marked a turning point in the cultural life of Florence with the coming to power of Lorenzo de' Medici and the success of the Careggi Academy, the flourishing sanctuary of Neoplatonism, which preached the glory of the artist and the hope of a new golden age.

Verrocchio's studio was therefore completely involved in this new age of poetry and naturalism, in which sculpture held sway over all the other arts. Turning away from the tormented dynamism of the Pollaiuolo brothers or the style of the followers of Desiderio da Settignano, Verrocchio proposed instead the cool equilibrium of his dreamy giant-killer, the solemnity of his ornamentation for the Medici tomb, or the finesse of his painted terracotta *Resurrection* (ca. 1470). In the works executed for the church, he obeyed the same principle of moderation in the large composition of *Christ and Saint Thomas* at Or' San Michele, or in *The Beheading of Saint John the Baptist* destined for the altar of the Baptistery in Florence.

The reputation of his studio in the field of sculpture spread far and wide. He collaborated on the *Funerary Monument of Cardinal Fortaguerri* in Pistoia, and Verrocchio's project was chosen in the contest for the *Equestrian Monument of Bartolomeo Colleoni*, in which movement is everything, and which was finished and inaugurated only in 1496 by Alessandro Leopardi. With the departure of Verrocchio and the Pollaiuolo brothers for Rome, Florence lost the supremacy in sculpture which it had held at the end of the Quattrocento.

Verrocchio's work and influence, however, were not limited to sculpture. His studio trained two of the greatest painters of the end of the 15th century, Lorenzo di Credi and Leonardo da Vinci, and left its mark on Italian art as a whole. His *Baptism of Christ*, painted between 1470 and 1480, is famous for including the first contribution of Leonardo da Vinci to painting: two angels whose fine modeling distinguishes them from the figures of Christ and John the Baptist. The pupil had already surpassed his master, having perfectly integrated his forms into space and invented the distant, dream-inducing landscape. While Lorenzo di Credi never went beyond the outmoded formulas of the Quattrocento, concentrating his efforts on clear forms and colors, polished surfaces and finish, Leonardo continued to

202

ANDREA DEL VERROCCHIO
David
(details)

Verrocchio's David was intended to be viewed from all sides, and has neither the anatomical complexity nor the psychological expressiveness of Donatello's version.

experiment and to increase his technical knowledge by participating in the production of the *bottega*. In 1481, he was given his first commission an *Adoration of the Magi* for the San Donato Monastery in Spoleto–the only major painting from his Florentine period still in existence. He demonstrated impressive power in his combination of forms and chiaroscuro handling. Still in 1481, summoned to the Sforza court, he left Florence to establish himself in Milan. His departure marked a turning point in the history of Italian art.

Sustained throughout the Quattrocento by the patronage of the Medici and other noble families, art flourished and made of Florence the cradle of the Renaissance. But by the end of the century new conditions were obtained. The period of serenity that had permitted the great artistic achievements was followed by a deep crisis both in the political and in the religious realms that led to the expulsion of the Medici in 1494. The cultural center of gravity shifted from Florence to Rome under the impetus of Pope Julius II, who re-established it as "capital of the world." Other cities like Venice and Milan also became important centers, however, and afforded favorable conditions for the creation of a new style. It was developed thanks to men like Leonardo and Michelangelo, both of whom were schooled in Florence, but whose artistic choices led directly into the next century.

ANDREA DEL VERROCCHIO
The Resurrection
ca. 1470, painted terracotta,
Museo Nazionale (Bargello),
Florence.

*The drawing and placing of the
angels, and the landscape
arrangement seem to have been
inspired by Luca della Robbia's own
version of this theme on the
tympanum of the door to the Sacristy
of Santa Maria del Fiore.
Verrocchio's realism is the more
powerful and striking of the two.*

207

ANDREA DEL VERROCCHIO
The Resurrection
(detail of Christ)

Opposite

ANDREA DEL VERROCCHIO
The Resurrection
(detail)

208

LEONARDO DA VINCI
The Adoration of the Magi
1482, wood, 246 x 243 cm.
Galleria degli Uffizi, Florence.

*In Verrocchio's studio, shortly before
leaving for Milan, Leonardo da
Vinci began working on an*
Adoration of the Magi—*it was
never finished. Although the work of
a young artist it represents a break
from the history of Quattrocento
painting. Leonardo organized his
composition according to different
pictorial zones: the foreground is
occupied only by the Virgin and
Child and other figures; the
background already stresses the
figurative importance of remote
horizons.*

LEONARDO DA VINCI
The Adoration of the Magi
(detail with staircase)

*Leonardo integrated into his
composition many of the pictorial
elements to be found in the works of
Quattrocento painters like Gozzoli
or Verrocchio (the palm tree), Piero
della Francesca (the orange tree), and
Lippi or Botticelli (the staircase).
The latter element has another
meaning here, however, it is the
means by which man can raise
himself above the tumult of the active
life (symbolized by horses).*

Opposite

LEONARDO DA VINCI
The Adoration of the Magi
(detail of Virgin and Child)
*As the makers of a new world, the
Virgin and Child occupy the center
of the composition.*

212

BERTOLDO DI GIOVANNI
Bellerophon and Pegasus
Before 1486, bronze, 32.5 cm.
Kunsthistorisches Museum,
Vienna

Florentine artists in Italy during the Quattrocento

AREZZO
Luca della Robbia (workshop)
Piero della Francesca
Giuliano da Maiano

BOLOGNA
Michelangelo Buonarroti
Andrea Sansovino

CORTONA
Fra Angelico

GENOA
Andrea Sansovino

LORETTO
Andrea Sansovino
Giuliano da Maiano
Giuliano da Sangallo

MANTUA
Leon Battista Alberti

MILAN
Leonardo da Vinci
Filarete
Michelozzo di Bartolomeo

NAPLES
Giuliano da Maiano

ORVIETO
Fra Angelico

PADUA
Donatello
Paolo Uccello
Fra Filippo Lippi

PAVIA
Filarete

PISA
Benozzo Gozzoli
Fra Bartolomeo

RIMINI
Leon Battista Alberti
Agostino di Duccio

ROME
Masolino da Panicale
Filarete
Bernardo Rossellino
Leon Battista Alberti
Donatello
Filippino Lippi
Antonio da Sangallo
Antonio Pollaiuolo
Piero Pollaiuolo

Fra Angelico
Sandro Botticelli
Domenico Ghirlandaio
Cosimo Roselli
Michelangelo Buonarroti

SIENA
Donatello
Lorenzo Ghiberti
Giuliano da Maiano

URBINO
Paolo Uccello
Luca della Robbia
Piero della Francesca

VENICE
Gentile da Fabriano
Paolo Uccello
Andrea del Castagno
Verrocchio

This list mentions only the major cities in which artists born in the 15th century worked. PRATO and PISTOIA are considered as being artistic satellites of Florence.

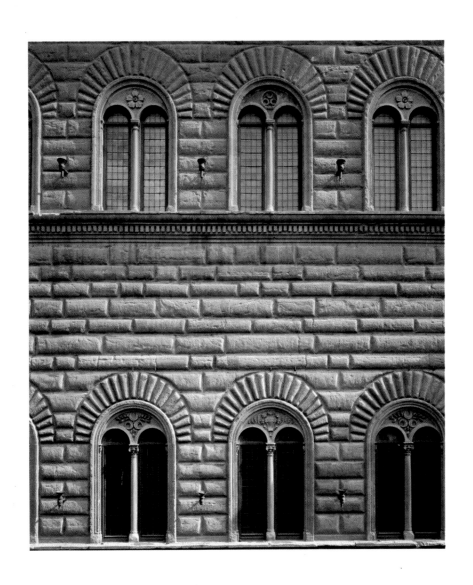

Giuliano da Maiano
Palazzo Strozzi
1489, Florence.

216

Selected

Bibliography

ALBERTI (L.B.), *De re aedificatoria*, Florence 1485.

ALBERTI (L.B.), *Zehn Bücher uber die Baukunst*, Vienna-Lepzig 1912

ALBERTI (L.B.), *De la statue et de la peinture*, Paris 1868.

ALBERTI (L.B.), *Della pittura*, critical edition by Luigi Mallé, Florence l950.

ARGAN (G.C.), *The Architecture of Brunelleschi and the Origins of Perspective Theory in the Fifteenth Century*, Journal of the Warburg and Courtauld Institutes, IX, London 1946.

ARGAN (G.C.), *Botticelli*, Geneva 1989.

AVERY (C.), *Florentine Renaissance Sculpture*. London 1970.

BALDINI (U.) and CASAZZA (0.), *The Brancacci Chapel*, Paris 1991.

BATTISTI (A.), *Piero della Francesca*, Milan 1971.

BAXANDALL (M.), *Painting and Experience in Fifteenth-century Italy*, Oxford 1974.

BAZIN (G.), *Fra Angelico*, Paris-London-New York 1949.

BEC (C.), *Les marchands écrivains*, Paris-The Hague 1967.

BERENSON (B.), *The Italian Pictures of the Renaissance Florentine School*, London 1963.

BERENSON (B.), *The Drawings of the Florentine Painters*, Chicago 1970.

BERTI (L.). *Catalogo del Museo Nazionale del Bargello*, Florence 1972.

BERTI (L.), and FOGGI (R.), *Masaccio,* Florence 1989.

Borsi (F.), Alberti. *Opera completa*, Milan 1975.

Burckhardt (J.), *La civilisation de la Renaissance en Italie*, Paris 1958.

Casazza (O.), *Masaccio e la Capella Brancacci*, Florence 1990.

Chambers (D.), *Patrons and Artists in the Italian Renaissance*, London 1970.

Chastel (A.), *Le Grand Atelier. 1460-1500.* Paris 1965.

Chastel (A.), *L'art italien*, Paris 1982.

Chastel (A.), *Mythe et crise de la Renaissance*, Geneva 1989.

Clark (K.), *Piero della Francesca. Complete Edition*, London 1969.

Damisch (H.), and Tongiorgi Tomasi (L.). *Paolo Uccello*, Paris 1996.

Degenhart (B.) and Schmitt (A.), *Gentile da Fabriano in Rom und die Anfänge des Antikenstudiums*, in Münchner Jahrbuch der bildenden Kunst, 11, 1960.

Filarete (A.), *Treatise on Architecture*, trans. John Spencer, New Haven 1965.

Focillon (H.), De Vecchi (P.), and Leonelli (M.C.), *Piero della Francesca*, Paris 1990.

Francastel (P.), *Peinture et société. Naissance et destruction d'un espace plastique, de la Renaissance au cubisme*, Paris 1977.

Francastel (P.), *La figure et le lieu. L'ordre visuel du Quattrocento*, Paris 1977.

Fremantle (R.), *Florentine Paintings in the Uffizi*, Florence 1971.

Gadel (J.), *Leon Battista Alberti,* Chicago-London 1989.

Ginsburg (C.), *Enquête sur Piero della Francesca.* Paris 1983.

Grassi (L.), *Donatello*, Paris 1969.

Hale (J.), *Italian Renaissance Painting,* London 1927.

Heydenreich (L.), *Eclosion de la Renaissance, 1400-1460*, Paris 1972.

Janson (H.), *The Sculpture of Donatello,* critical catalogue, Princeton 1957.

Leonardo da Vinci, *Traité de la peinture*, Paris 1964.

Lerner-Lehmkuhl (H.), *Zur Struktur und Geschichte des Florentitinischen Kunstmarktes im 15. Jahrhundert.* Wattenscheid 1936.

Longhi (R.), *Piero della Francesca*, Florence 1964.

Lunardi (R.), *Arte e Storia in Santa Maria Novella*, Florence 1983.

Mandel, (L.), *L'opera completa del Botticelli*, Milan 1967.

Marcucci (L.), *Gallerie Nazionali di Firenze. I dipinti toscani del secolo XIV*, Rome 1965.

Meiss (M.), *The Great Age of Fresco, Discoveries. Recoveries and Survivals,* London 1970.

Moranti (E.) and Baldini (U.), *Angelico,* Milan 1970.

Orlandi (S.), *Beato Angelico*, Florence 1964.

Piero della Francesca, *De prospectiva pingendi* (1480?), Florence 1942 .

Pope-Henessy (J.), *La peinture siennoise du Quattrocento*, Paris 1947.

Pope-Henessy (J.), *Angelico*, London 1952.

Pope-Henessy (J.), *Paolo Uccello. Complete edition,* London 1969.

Procacci (U.), Baldini (U.) and Berti (L.), *Fresques de Florence* (catalogue), Paris 1970.

Ragghianti, *Filippo Brunelleschi*, Florence 1977.

Salmi (M.), *Fra Angelico*, Paris 1973.

Seymour (C.), *Sculpture in Italy, 1400 to 1500*, Harmondsworth 1966.

Sindona (E.), *Introduzione alla poetica di Paolo Uccello. Relazioni tra prospettiva e pensiero teorico,* in l'Arte, 1972.

Steinberg (R.), *Fra Girolamo Savonarola. Florentine Art and Renaissance Bibliography,* Athens, Ohio, 1977.

Venturi (L.), *Piero della Francesca*, Geneva 1954.

Index
of the main italian artists
and their works

Printed in Italy by La Zincografica Fiorentina